Pulling Together

*Integrating inquiry, assessment, and instruction
in today's English classroom*

LEYTON SCHNELLERT

MEHJABEEN DATOO

KRISTA EDIGER

JOANNE PANAS

Pembroke Publishers Limited

Dedication

To the students, mentors, and colleagues who inspire us to pull things apart.

Acknowledgments

Nothing done well is ever done alone. We would like to acknowledge and gratefully thank the teachers who worked with us on the classroom examples included in this book, for their expertise, time, and willingness to share: Lisa Cooke, Sue Gall, Julie Anne Mainville, Andrea Matza, Catriona Misfeldt, Alecia Payne, Rebeca Rubio, Erin Steele, Tracy Sullivan, Baren Tsui, and Nicole Widdess. We would also like to thank the teacher-researchers who have significantly influenced our thinking: Nancie Atwell, Kylene Beers, Faye Brownlie, Deborah Butler, Carl Leggo, Jill McClay, Bob Probst, Cris Tovani, and Jeff Wilhelm. Thanks, also, to Pembroke Publishers' Mary Macchiusi, for giving the four of us an opportunity to write together, and Kat Mototsune, our editor, for her thoughtful reading of the manuscript. Finally, we want to acknowledge the support we have received from Richmond School District's many professional learning communities, in particular our colleagues from eight years of Richmond's Strengthening Student Literacy Network, where it all began.

© 2009 Pembroke Publishers
538 Hood Road
Markham, Ontario, Canada L3R 3K9
www.pembrokepublishers.com

Distributed in the U.S. by Stenhouse Publishers
480 Congress Street
Portland, ME 04101
www.stenhouse.com

We acknowledge the financial support of the Government of Canada through the Book Publishing Industry Development Program (BPIDP) for our publishing activities.

We acknowledge the assistance of the Government of Ontario through the Ontario Media Development Corporation's Ontario Book Initiative.

Library and Archives Canada Cataloguing in Publication

Pulling together : planning inquiry, curriculum, and assessment for better instruction in English classroom / Leyton Schnellert ... [et al.].

Includes bibliographical references and index.
ISBN 978-1-55138-237-1

1. English language—Study and teaching (Secondary). 2. English language—Study and teaching (Elementary). 3. Language arts (Secondary). 4. Language arts (Elementary). I. Schnellert, Leyton

LB1575.8.P84 2009   428.0071'2   C2009-902720-8

Editor: Kat Mototsune
Cover Design: John Zehethofer
Typesetting: Jay Tee Graphics Ltd.

Printed and bound in Canada
9 8 7 6 5 4 3 2 1

FSC
Mixed Sources
Product group from well-managed
forests and other controlled sources
Cert no. SW-COC-002358
www.fsc.org
© 1996 Forest Stewardship Council

Contents

Introduction: Pulling Together Principles and Practices

Who would have thought that the four of us would write a book together? We come from such different backgrounds, our journeys have been so disparate, and yet we have come to share many of the same beliefs and practices about teaching and about teaching language arts. When we began teaching we had big ideas about the meaning of teaching; we wondered about how to empower human beings and break down power structures—how to have an impact in the world through the classroom. Our collaboration began at a time when we were feeling the need to examine how our practice was moving us toward or pulling us away from these overarching goals. We came together around issues of assessment, diversity, and the teaching of strategies. We wondered how to teach so students actually improve over time, and how to plan for that. In the end, we realized that all these questions were addressed through the idea of coherence— how all the different parts work together to create a classroom that makes sense for us and for our students.

We have a shared set of goals as English language arts teachers. We want students to feel connected to the community we create in the classroom and to have the tools to connect to, analyze, and respond to the world. We want them to be passionate about what they are learning and to see how it is relevant. Passionate learning is about engagement and being able to extend learning beyond the classroom, about searching for knowledge without placing limits on what will be learned, about being open, and about wanting to deeply understand.

We have noticed five characteristics of passionate, engaged learning:

1. First and foremost, passionate learning is rooted in deep engagement.
2. Openness of mind is essential to passionate learning.
3. Students feel a sense of connection between what they are learning and themselves, their communities, and beyond.
4. Students feel that what they are learning is connecting to and enhancing/transforming what they already know.
5. Passionate learning develops a sense of agency.

Passionate learning is rooted in deep engagement. We want kids to be intrigued, to be excited, and to sustain that over time; we want them to be moved and we want to move them forward as learners. We want them to ask questions and to develop ways of looking for and considering ideas that lead to richer and deeper understandings: this kind of thinking is at the heart of English language arts. We use the inquiry process to support students in building their thinking through the exploration of concepts. These efforts encourage independent, passionate learners and thinkers who persevere through a variety of challenges to deeper conceptual understandings.

How This Book Is Organized

In the first three chapters, we outline the principles and practices that shape our planning and teaching. The chapters that follow become more specific: they include detailed lesson sequences and units that demonstrate how we have integrated assessment, planning, and instruction in our classrooms. In each chapter, we start with an introduction to our thinking and list our core understandings, and follow with examples from our classrooms and those of our colleagues. Chapters 4, 5, and 6 focus on the "big three" of language arts: oral language, reading, and writing. Chapters 7, 8, and 9 explore new literacies, critical literacy, and integrated units.

In this book, we pull together many of the teaching practices that we have explored and played with over the years. Many of our units are organized around inquiry questions; we also use the principles of backwards design. We consistently use three structures throughout our planning and instruction: explicitly teaching thinking skills, gradually releasing responsibility to students, and assessing both formatively and summatively. Metacognition is also key, as is teaching for the diversity of learners in our classes. You will see instructional approaches such as literature/text circles, strategic teaching, arts-based learning, apprenticeship, cooperative learning, and differentiation. Throughout, you will find an emphasis on the process of learning and thinking, supported and situated in the classroom. We explore these ideas throughout the book, demonstrating how they can be incorporated into practice as a way to build engagement, develop thinking, and move students to independence.

With this book, we invite you into conversation about ways to remain deeply engaged as teachers and to develop a passion for learning in your students. Our journey to deepen our practice, as well as the engagement of our students, is far from over. This book is a chance for us to synthesize and represent our current thinking; underneath it lies a messy and iterative process.

Yours in teaching and learning,
Leyton, Mehjabeen, Krista, and Joanne

CHAPTER 1

Working Together to Build Practices

Teaching can be a solitary act. It takes time to meet with other educators to discuss teaching and learning, and we all know how little time remains after a full day of classes, a lunch meeting, and a briefcase of marking. Discussions with other educators around teaching and learning do not, however, rob us of time. They sustain us; they make more valuable the time we spend teaching.

Each of us has arrived at this conclusion: collaboration is necessary to our survival as teachers. We share our struggles and listen to concerns. Simply knowing we'll be spending time with people who have similar questions and tensions provides support. We value connecting with one another—together we create a place where we can relax, maybe complain a bit, and then move on to restorative conversation and work.

Collaboration can have a significant positive impact on the learning in our classrooms and schools.

The four of us have worked and continue to work with many different groups of educators. Our collaboration as a group of four is enriched by the work we do with others, including those in the original district study group where we met. Cross-pollination occurs through the myriad interactions we have with students, colleagues, and mentors. Talking together encourages us to explain why we do what we do; we become more informed when we collaborate. We can confidently take this knowledge and articulation into our work with others.

Finding Ways to Work Together

Although we have had some successful collaborative experiences, these tended to be project-based, and we wanted to have a sustained collaborative community despite the fact that we all worked at different sites. Our individual desires to investigate two or three topics in depth led us to the realization that we needed to meet regularly to have the space and time to share, discuss, create, problem-solve, and plan together. We needed a way to delve deeply into the issues and practices that mattered to us the most, to see the bigger structures across the year and reporting periods, across our philosophies and styles.

Working together helps us be more reflective, responsive, adaptive, and intentional. It helps us to engage deeply in our practice. When everyone knows why we are doing what we are doing, both in our classrooms with our students and in our planning, our work becomes more refined and purposeful, our actions more aligned with our goals. We see more success.

Over the last five years, we have met together regularly to discuss a variety of topics, including literature for both ourselves and our students, relevant professional resources, and big ideas and issues related to teaching and education. Our collaborative inquiry is driven by our desire to improve classroom practice. Therefore what is discussed is also linked to the realities of our classrooms, our students, and our practice. Perhaps the most holistic or integrated activity we do is plan units together, which we adapt to the different grades and students we teach. We wrestle with theory and practice; this work propels us forward and

It can seem at times as though we accomplish less in terms of tangible markers than we might when working alone, but our conversations clarify our ideas, forcing us to clarify them for our students.

We find we learn best when we are able to try things out and reflect on them together. This allows us to practice and support each other as we struggle with implementing approaches that are outside our comfort zone. Team teaching provides a rich opportunity for students, as well; having two teachers in a room gives us the time and scope to address the diversity of our students' needs.

outward to share what we have with our colleagues, who take it and make it their own, then share it back with us and with others.

While we often create materials for individual lessons, the major focus of our unit planning involves the development of inquiry questions, text sets, and formative and summative assessments. We challenge each other to ensure that we are teaching something engaging, with enough scaffolding to meet the needs of a diverse group of students. We end up leaving these sessions with a clear idea of where we're going—a framework for our unit. Often, we will plan an anchor lesson sequence together—it is a chance to pool our energies into something new we are trying to develop. Having our shared thinking to refer to, we find that building the rest of our lesson sequences becomes an enjoyable and manageable task.

By collaboration, we don't mean that we teach identical lessons. When we plan a unit together, although our inquiry question may be the same, the lessons themselves look different in each of our classrooms. While we create a framework for the unit together, we pace and adapt our lessons with our specific classes in mind. We love to work together, but we also have such varied teaching styles and strengths that the lessons we deliver are often very different. Our diversity supports us in developing our ideas and practice in order to better meet the diverse needs of our students.

An exciting component of our collaboration is the variety of text sets we're able to collect for each unit we plan together, which is a way to differentiate instruction. We most often develop inquiry units around a theme, and together we're able to brainstorm enough novel titles for a literature circle to span a wide range of reading levels and interests. Together, we work to complement literature circles with print, visual, and multimodal texts.

There is a natural progression from collaborative planning with colleagues to collaborative planning with students. The more we work together to build units, the more we look to our students to co-construct the curriculum with us. We strongly believe in involving students in determining and reflecting on what we are doing and learning. Together, we are engaged in developing the practices of speaking, listening, reading, viewing, writing, and representing. Students become curriculum makers as we include them in the assessment and planning process. We find that collaboration of all kinds works best when we are open to and comfortable with discomfort, ambiguity, messing around with other ideas, revising practices and plans, responding to feedback, and weaving in different perspectives. Key to collaboration is the ongoing questioning and reflection that both teachers and students do to determine where we are going, what we are getting better at, what needs to be revisited.

Re-Imagining English Language Arts: Our Perspective

English language arts (ELA) curricula require that we develop students' thinking and communication skills. When this is done while keeping our students' passions, interests, and strengths in mind, it can become a way for them to better understand and experience the world. We're clear about our goal—we want to create classrooms of passionate, deeply engaged learners. By re-imagining what ELA can look like, we design approaches to do just that.

Learning in English Language Arts

We want to help students in our ELA classrooms broaden and deepen their understanding of themselves, others, life, and the world. We believe that the most powerful way to do this is by working together with students to develop and explore ideas and practices. We read and write in order to explore, pass on, and critique ideas and values. Ideas in all disciplines move us forward; the discipline of language arts moves us forward through and with reflection at both the individual and societal levels.

In the ELA classroom, we consider what is necessary to live in and contribute to a healthy society. The problems addressed by the discipline include looking closely and critically at who we are as individuals, communities, and nations; gaining insight into ourselves and making changes (or not); and creating rich and worthy lives by learning through literature and other texts—because we cannot possibly learn it all through direct experience. Learning in English language arts is about reading and creating a variety of texts that examine the world, with all its beauty and flaws, and deciding for ourselves what it means to live and act in the world.

One of the important things we explore with our students is the range of texts from which we can make meaning. In our classrooms, all forms of text are welcome. By introducing a variety of texts to our students and inviting them to bring in their own, we create a context within which they can develop their skills and strategies in authentic and meaningful ways.

Our task as teachers is to build the capacity of every student to understand, respond to, analyze, and create texts. Every student has some experience in these areas, and every student has plenty of room to grow. We want students to expand their repertoire of techniques and strategies, and to develop their capacity to purposefully and flexibly use language. We want students to speak and write both directly and metaphorically, to analyze, choose, and harness the power of language.

These are broad aims. In order to meet them we need to know our goals for our students before we can effectively plan units of study. We use formative assessment to ensure that we are achieving these goals. To that end, we must continually ask ourselves if our students are actually thinking and learning, and what we need to do differently in order to help them.

Thinking in English Language Arts

How can we know that students are thinking when they are reading? We can't see their minds at work, so we must rely on their behaviors—are they deeply engrossed in the text, almost undistractable? Are they holding their thinking about it somehow, by posing questions, recording connections, or noting significant quotations and their thoughts about them? If we interrupt their reading, can they summarize what they've read? Can they make some inferences, or ask thoughtful questions? Can they have passionate, articulate conversations about what they are reading? Will they accept viewpoints other than their own, or be open to multiple interpretations? Do they reread portions of text to confirm or refute their own viewpoints or those of others? When they demonstrate these behaviors, students are thinking, and thinking hard, about that text.

Similarly, how can we know that a student is thinking about a concept or big idea? Perhaps we have been reading and talking in class about the concept of truth; can the student develop insights about truth in his or her own life, based on his or her own values and beliefs? Can the student think critically about truth in different arenas: history, science, advertising? Can the student write a story or poem that says something significant about the meaning of truth, or the importance of telling the truth? If the student is able to do these things, it shows that the student has been thinking a great deal and come to some understandings about the concept of truth.

We know our students have learned something when they

- get better at a skill over time; for example
  - reading closely/thoughtfully
  - discussing texts and topics critically and insightfully
  - creating and revising a variety of texts
  - choosing, using, creating, and adapting strategies for these skills
- pull together ideas/concepts from a variety of texts (synthesize); for example
  - using various texts to speak/write about or represent a concept
  - putting together various concepts to create a new concept or idea
- apply acquired strategies and approaches to new situations; for example
  - finding themes in a poem using a strategy for finding themes in a story
  - using symbolism in a representation of their learning
  - using methods for holding thinking in their independent novels
  - thinking critically about their own beliefs and values
- engage in metacognition and self-regulation; for example
  - reflecting on their methods and learning
  - engaging in self-assessment and goal-setting
  - adjusting methods to be more successful in their learning

Strategies for Success in English Language Arts

In order to achieve the ends listed above, we teach students various strategies to give them the cognitive tools necessary to become better thinkers and communicators. Reading and viewing, writing and representing, speaking and listening are all thinking processes. The discipline of English language arts promotes critical thinking and analysis, as well as personal expression. The skills of language arts include reading critically and thoughtfully; responding to literature on a personal level and through the eyes of others, thereby gaining multiple perspectives; and communicating ideas and thoughts. Another way to look at the skills and strategies of language arts is through the lenses of comprehension, response and analysis, composition, and self-regulation.

Comprehension
- Activating prior knowledge
- Predicting
- Developing questions
- Making connections
- Inferring
- Building schema
- Visualizing
- Determining importance
- Using fix-up strategies to repair meaning
- Organizing information
- Summarizing
- Synthesizing
- Applying

Response and Analysis
- Responding personally
- Considering audience and purpose
- Perspective-taking
- Identifying bias
- Making reasoned judgments

Composition

- Identifying a purpose and audience
- Generating ideas
- Choosing appropriate forms
- Organizing ideas
- Drafting
- Elaborating
- Developing voice and style
- Revising

Self-Regulation

- Interpreting tasks
- Setting a purpose
- Self-assessing and setting goals
- Reflecting on own thinking
- Using feedback
- Adjusting approaches

In the chapters of this book we share examples of teaching practices that we use to help students develop their thinking and understanding of concepts. Each of the strategies and skills mentioned here needs to be explicitly taught and developed over time. Just as we need to develop practices that we can use in multiple ways, our students need to develop thinking practices they can use and adapt in multiple contexts. Our ultimate goal is student ownership and independence.

CHAPTER 2

Integrating Planning, Assessment, and Instruction

We need to be open-minded to our students' ideas and experiences if we want students to be open to what they learn in our classrooms.

To inspire passion and engagement, we have moved to the inquiry process in our classrooms; which allows us to better incorporate our students' strengths, stretches, and interests so that we can build understandings and thinking strategies together. We begin our lessons and units by asking students what they already know and believe about ideas, texts, and approaches; from the very beginning, students are involved in the process of building connections and making meaning.

Inquiry units require students to challenge and extend their understandings by asking questions, interpreting a variety of texts, and personalizing and transforming their understandings of themselves and the world. Ultimately, we want students to build a sense of connection between themselves, each other, and the communities in which they live. For their interactions and understandings to go beyond the surface, students must develop an openness of mind to hear, identify, and link a number of perspectives and ideas. We want students to allow these new ideas and perspectives to connect with and shift their conceptual understandings.

To support deep and engaged learning, we develop performance tasks that allow students to demonstrate the understandings and approaches that they have acquired during the course of a unit. The skills and understandings that they have acquired become tools for them to apply beyond that unit of study and the classroom.

Rethinking Thematic Teaching

We may have planned a thematic unit on power and corruption using *Macbeth*, *The Crucible*, and *Lord of the Flies* as core texts, with a final comparative essay on this theme. Embedded within the expectations for the essay were a number of reading, writing, and thinking skills; students may have written satisfactory essays, but were they getting better at these thinking and writing skills? And did those skills have any connection to the big thematic ideas we had explored throughout the unit?

For many years, we designed our units around themes, and found this an inclusive and interesting way to engage students in our classrooms. We were able to talk about the big ideas, but we found that thematic teaching in itself didn't develop specific skills and competencies in students. Even when we addressed particular skills and strategies, students often did not use or apply them in other units. Thematic teaching didn't require that we identify up front the skills and strategies that our students needed in order to demonstrate development or competence by the end of the unit. We clearly needed a different planning process, one that combined thematic teaching, strategic teaching, and backwards design.

In English language arts we tend to generate two kinds of big ideas related to

1. language processes (i.e., how to understand and communicate), and
2. larger themes around the human experience.

A performance task is a complex activity that goes beyond recall and asks students to synthesize and demonstrate their learning. The nature of the task is open-ended, so that students can show their understanding of a concept or idea and demonstrate their competency with the skills and strategies we have been targeting.

Designing our units around both kinds of big ideas enables students to make connections to what they know and believe, and develop ways to further understand and act in the world. We believe English language arts is about exploring big ideas while developing the practices of the discipline. Identifying these big ideas, framing them as questions, and sharing these overarching questions with students helps us link teaching and learning activities back to a shared purpose.

In our planning process, we develop inquiry questions that relate to big ideas and that engage our students' interest. Wiggins and McTighe (2000) and Wilhelm (2007) talk about students developing enduring understandings that are neither facts nor details but rather overarching ideas that can be explored through a variety of learning activities. During the course of a unit we ask students to show how their understandings are developing by using many formative assessments (collecting evidence about students' learning to guide our teaching) and a few performance tasks, which we use for our summative assessments.

PULLING TOGETHER PRACTICES

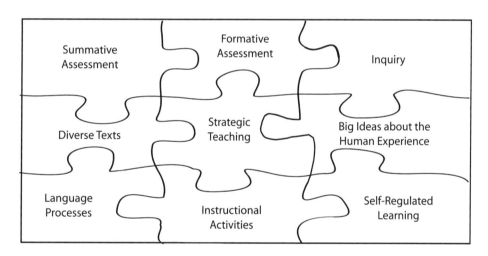

While it would be easy to suggest that we start with the big ideas, then move to the assessment, followed by instructional activities, the reality is that sometimes we start with the texts, other times we start with a big idea, and often we begin with a language process (i.e., thinking skill) that our formative assessment shows our students need to work on. It does not matter where we begin our planning as long as each component is included.

In our work with each other and with other colleagues, we find that everyone engages in the planning process from different entry points but that, as we keep working through our ideas and suggestions, the coherence develops and holds together the diversity of our contributions.

We find that teaching using inquiry questions helps students to get at big ideas using a process of meaning-making through discovery. To begin, we formatively assess our students to help us choose a few key thinking skills that support the development of the big ideas. For example, in a unit on Children of the World we co-planned for Humanities 8, one of the big ideas was perspective. The thinking skills we chose to develop in this unit were visualization and inference. We first helped students develop complex and detailed images that synthesized information from a range of texts, as a way for them to expand their thinking. We practiced these skills with our literature circle novels by having students draw pictures to summarize what they read and to help them empathize with the characters' experiences. We then taught them to take information from a variety of visual texts like images, maps, and statistical tables, and use it to make inferences about life in other parts of the world. Visualization skills helped our students better understand the experiences and context of other children in the world.

Big ideas are more than goals for a unit or grade; they are the rationale for engaging in ELA. Learning with big ideas in mind engages students in the purposeful and strategic use of thinking strategies. To determine our big ideas for a unit, we brainstorm themes based on our students' background knowledge and interests, the texts we know and have, what's happening in the world, and concepts in other curriculum areas.

For example, one summer we were intrigued by a novel called *Fish*. What excited us about this book was that it is told from the point of view of a child living in an unnamed, conflict- and drought-ridden country; we never learn the gender, age, or nationality of the child narrator. This offers students the opportunity to interpret and share what they see in the text. What a great place to begin a year—with a text that could allow us to ask our students to identify what assumptions they are making about the character and setting, and to help them trace where these assumptions might come from. At the same time, the text offers us a window into the challenges of surviving in a time of conflict and the resources required to do so. The themes that emerge from this text for us are the roles of hope, knowledge, and friendship in survival. It certainly speaks to our students as they try to survive their first year of high school.

To determine language-process outcomes that complement the thematic big ideas we are exploring in a given unit, we look to the ELA curriculum. We recognize that going deeply into a few thinking skills, rather than trying to "cover it all" within a unit, can have a significant impact on student learning. The ambiguity in *Fish* inspired many questions. The novel also painted very vivid pictures in our minds. Therefore, the thinking skills we chose to focus on and summatively assess for the survival unit were questioning, visualization, and representing ideas with images. A core skill that students need to develop and use throughout high school and their lives is the ability to support their ideas with evidence; therefore another key skill we chose was writing with evidence. Through the unit, we also introduced students to and formatively assessed the skills of making connections and writing personal responses, which became focus areas for the following unit.

See page 20 for a reproducible template of the organizer we use for unit planning.

SAMPLE ORGANIZER FOR UNIT PLANNING: SURVIVAL THEME

Unit Focus/Theme: Survival

Inquiry Questions	How is hope, knowledge, or friendship necessary for the survival of the human spirit? In the novel you read, is hope, knowledge, or friendship most important for the survival of the character's spirit?
Shared Text	*Fish* by L.S. Matthews

Literature Circle Texts	*Gathering Blue, Speak, Tomorrow, When the War Began, House of the Scorpion, The Edge, Max the Mighty, Stuck in Neutral, Julie of the Wolves, Deathwatch, Invitation to the Game, Night, The Wreckers, The Tunnel King, The Wind Singer, Parvana's Journey, Forbidden City, Mud City, The Garbage King, Theories of Relativity*
Writing Genre/Types	Impromptu writing (quickwrites, response journals) The beginnings of literary analysis
Writing/Representing Strategies (language processes)	Coherence (staying on topic) Using quotations and specific evidence and explanations Representing ideas graphically
Reading/Viewing Strategies (language processes)	Activating prior knowledge Questioning Visualization
Instructional Activities	Quickwrites Think-Alouds Say Something Three-Way Interview Twenty Questions
Formative Assessment	Descriptive feedback Criteria building Self- and peer assessment
Summative Assessment	Reading journal Character Survival Kit: Summative assignment that tracks thinking and deals with the essential question related to survival

Strategic Teaching

At the core of our planning and teaching processes is the students' simultaneous exploration of big ideas and development of thinking skills. In order to develop these, we incorporate purposeful and explicit instruction, a process often referred to as strategic teaching (Wilhelm, 2001). As we begin to focus on planning our actual lesson sequences, we are careful to keep in mind the big ideas—both thematic and process-based—of the unit, and to choose instructional techniques to complement the goals we have for our students.

Gradual Release

One of the most important words in our teaching vocabulary is "how." In English language arts, students need to know how to do a wide variety of skills and processes. If we are too focused on *what* students need to know—and the list can be large: the essay, the elements of literature, literary devices, genres of literature, the writing process—it can be easy to lose sight of the *how*. If we think of these *whats* in terms of *hows*, our task as educators becomes clearer:

- How do you write an essay?
- How do you use the elements of literature to understand a story or movie?
- How do writers use literary devices to get their ideas across?
- How do you know what genre a piece of text is?
- How do you make the writing process work for you?

On closer inspection, it becomes clear that many of these *how* questions can be broken down into even more *how* questions:

How do you write an essay? might become

- How do you choose a topic for an essay?
- How do you generate and organize ideas?
- How do you write an engaging introduction?
- How do you explain your ideas clearly and integrate support for them?
- How do you write a strong conclusion?

How do you use the elements of literature to understand a story or movie? might become

- How do you identify the elements of literature in a story or movie?
- How do authors decide what elements to use or emphasize?
- How do authors use the elements to get across their big ideas?
- How are the elements used differently in short stories, novels, plays, and movies?
- How do you interpret and explain the use of an element in a text?

What we are really talking about here is the thinking tasks that we do automatically and expertly, and which we sometimes assume that our students are able to do. However, when you look at exactly what it is we are asking students to do, it becomes clear that these are very complex tasks that need to be taught. In other words, we need to make the invisible, silent, implicit thinking tasks we do visible, audible, and explicit.

One of the best ways to do this is to use the process of *gradual release of responsibility* (Pearson & Gallagher, 1983).

"Gradual release of responsibility is an instructional process whereby a teacher models a concept or strategy and makes explicit the thinking one engages in when choosing and applying that strategy in a specific context. Gradually students are given more independence with the goal of being able to use the strategy on their own" (BC Ministry of Education, 2007: 93).

This process can happen over a single class block, or it may take multiple opportunities and much practice to get students to where they can do the task purely independently; at that stage, they will have internalized, personalized, and taken ownership of the task or strategy, and should be able to adapt and/or transfer it to other tasks or areas.

Another way of thinking about gradual release is to use these four steps (Wilhelm, Baker & Dube Hackett, 2001: 11):

1. I do, you watch.
2. I do, you help.
3. You do, I help.
4. You do, I watch.

In this way, students are "apprenticed" into the discipline of English language arts, much like a plumber or carpenter might teach an apprentice their trade. Notice that the two middle steps are the teacher and students working together on the actual task; gradual release goes beyond modeling, beyond a demonstration, and beyond explicit detailed instructions—it's about doing it *together*.

Below, we outline a gradual release process for reaching students to generate lines for a first draft of a free verse poem. The teacher has already done an activity with students to generate and narrow topics for the poem, and has enlisted the help of another teacher (e.g. a resource teacher, an administrator, a librarian, or a teacher on a prep block—or senior students on their spares, or even a willing student from the class, provided you give them some time to prepare).

1. I do, you watch

- In preparation, the teacher asks the partner teacher to help brainstorm ideas for a poem about the teacher's brother.
- In class, the partner asks the teacher to tell about her brother; as they talk, the teacher is prompted by her partner to write down interesting details in short lines on strips of chart paper: e.g., "That's funny—write that down!"; "I like that description of his hair."
- The partner asks the teacher some probing and clarifying questions: e.g., "What were you fighting about?"; "Why was it hard to give him a hug?" The teacher writes down her answers on the strips of paper.
- After a few minutes of this, the teacher turns to the students and asks them to tell what they saw the two partners doing. Students tell back their observations.

2. I do, you help

- After the students report what they saw, they are given the opportunity to help the teacher as she continues to brainstorm ideas—the *students* are now the teacher's partner.
- The (former) partner supports the students as they think of ways to help the teacher generate more interesting details about her brother.
- At this point, students might also be asked to help the teacher arrange the lines on strips of chart paper in various ways, a task they will be asked to do with their own partners later in the process. Alternatively, the task of arranging ideas could become another round of modeling and gradual release, depending on the needs of the particular group of students.

3. You do, I help

- Once students have had sufficient practice time, the teacher and partner give the class some feedback on how well they helped the teacher generate ideas, and offer suggestions as to what they might do better.
- The teacher might also write up the tasks of each partner as they take turns with the roles of writer and helper.
- Students pair up and begin the process of generating ideas for their own poems with each other.
- The teacher helps by circulating, observing, listening, quietly interjecting when a pair seems to be having trouble, and pausing the class (perhaps before switching tasks or partners) to make some general comments on what's working and what needs work.

4. You do, I watch

- Once students have had a chance to see, to help, and to try, and have gotten some feedback, they can proceed on their own.
- This is a good time for the teacher to continue observing as students work without interruption (except where problems or questions arise that students can't deal with).

At the end of the student activity, one way to formatively assess learning is for students to write a brief self-evaluation:

- What worked, what needs work, and what they will do next time they work with a partner to generate ideas, using the list of tasks generated earlier?
- How might they adapt the strategy for use in generating ideas for an essay or another task?

With gradual release, we engage students in examining the thinking skills and approaches we introduce; together we reflect on how these processes work, why they are helpful, and how they might be adapted or applied in other situations.

Gradual release works well with any strategy, skill, or process that you might use in the discipline of ELA and beyond: comprehension strategies, note-making, inferring, analysis of any text, any writing process, even group discussion skills. It results in students who have a very clear idea not only of the process they are engaging in but of expectations for performance. It lends itself beautifully to generating criteria for the task, as well as to metacognition and self-regulation of that task. We find this approach to gradual release an indispensable tool to help our students understand on a deep level *how* to do any aspect of thinking and learning.

Self-Regulated Learning

Self-regulating learners define expectations; set goals; select, adapt, or invent learning strategies; self-monitor outcomes; and revise goals or approaches to learning in order to achieve desired outcomes (Butler & Schnellert, 2008).

Self-regulation is an important concept that we use to help remind us of our end-goal for our students. We want our students to be able to determine what thinking and language processes an activity requires of them, and then to identify and use approaches that will help them successfully develop and communicate their ideas and understandings. In our classrooms, self-regulated learning includes asking students to set goals and monitor their attempts to reach these goals.

At the heart of self-regulation is metacognition. Metacognition is "thinking about thinking," which results in increased understanding of one's own learning processes. When students become aware of their thinking processes, their ability to take responsibility for and control over their learning increases. Think of what students need to do to be successful within an inquiry project: they have to actively construct goals or questions and then plan their inquiry, and frequently check to see if the methods they are using are working; if not, they need to change what they are doing. By thinking about how they think and learn, students gain control over the strategies they use.

The reflective planning that the four of us have done together and with other colleagues over recent years mirrors the metacognitive processes we use to stimulate thinking in our classrooms. When we step back with our colleagues and our students to determine what is most important for us to work on, we harness our energy to make progress on something specific.

But just thinking about one's thinking is not enough. We want students to act on reflections about their learning. Too often we have put metacognitive activities at the *end* of a unit, when students are no longer deeply immersed in the process of creating and making meaning. So we shifted our focus to getting students involved in assessing and adapting what they do within longer units of study, where the same key skills are used and developed over time. As we want students to be more successful in communicating their thoughts and ideas, we get them inside the processes of reading, writing, speaking, and listening by collaboratively analyzing, generating, and/or working with criteria *during* a unit of study and while they are reading or composing longer texts. When teachers and students work together to identify what's needed in order to successfully complete a task, students become engaged in learning that is both meaningful and purposeful.

In order for students to understand how they think about and can successfully approach tasks, they need to be able to determine and describe what tasks require of them. Published work, student exemplars, and existing criteria can be used to fuel discussions about task demands and requirements. It is even more beneficial for students to be involved in the development of criteria for tasks, including the kinds of strategies that might be used and descriptions of how to tell whether strategies have been used effectively. By analyzing tasks and the strategies needed for success, students are constructing an understanding of what is needed to fully meet expectations. Through this construction they are able to take ownership of their learning and to adapt and modify their strategies and approaches as a context requires.

In this book we share examples of classroom "assessment as learning" activities embedded within lessons and units. These include performance-based assessments, class and individual goal-setting activities, and student-generated criteria as they pertain to reading, writing, and oral language activities.

Organizer for Unit Planning

Unit Focus/Theme:	
Inquiry Questions	
Shared Text(s)	
Literature/Information Circle Texts	
Writing Genre/Types	
Writing/Representing Strategies (language processes)	
Reading/Viewing Strategies (language processes)	
Instructional Activities	
Formative Assessment	
Summative Assessment	

CHAPTER 3

Responsive Teaching and Assessment

We had found ways of bringing students into the process of diagnostic assessment by sharing our results in different ways: Krista often wrote letters to her classes speaking to the trends that she saw in their writing; Mehjabeen had her students track her assessment of their skills and set personal goals, while explicitly sharing her class goals and linking them to what she was teaching on a given day; Joanne often began the year by having students write a personal piece that allowed her to both assess their writing abilities and get to know them; Leyton had students create personal portfolios that represented aspects of themselves as learners.

We are deeply committed to having community-minded classrooms where students have voice and choice. Our journey to become more responsive teachers is steeped in the recognition that learners need opportunities to build from their interests and from what they know and can do. Students come into our classes with many abilities, competencies, passions, insecurities, and hopes. We continually try to unearth and understand the complexity of students' experiences and development.

The notion of doing classroom diagnostic assessments with our students was not a new one for most of us; for years, we had been having students in our classes begin the year with a writing task that helped inform us of their strengths and gave us a sense of what we had to teach them. Having clarity about our students' strengths allowed us to make thoughtful decisions about what we needed to teach in a given year, and kept us focused on specific goals. It also helped students to find value in what we were doing as they were able to see how our teaching was aimed at developing their abilities in an explicit way.

Performance-Based Assessment

A common practice of assessment that occurs in schools is a grade-wide assessment of student writing. Students in a particular grade are given a task that is scored by a team of teachers, in order to provide insight into the strengths of students. In the schools we were working in, this assessment sometimes occurred midway through the school year or at the end. The data was used as part of students' grades, in an effort to "standardize" assessment. While teachers found value in the process of collaborative scoring, the second step of thinking together, building from the results to plan instruction was not a formal or common part of the process. What we assess are the thinking skills we value; from this formative assessment we choose a few key areas that we think will make the most difference for our students and their learning.

We have worked to bring together the two practices of classroom diagnostic assessment and grade-wide assessment. In our schools we now engage in grade-wide assessments of students' reading skills. Working in teams, teachers develop a performance-based assessment (PBA) that shows us what reading abilities and strategies students bring with them into secondary school. We base our PBA on work by Faye Brownlie (1998, 2006, 2009). The PBA (see page 35) is collaboratively scored by teachers, who then work together to set goals for their classes and develop common strategies or areas of focus across subjects. The value of this assessment process is that it allows us to gain insight into our students' strengths at the beginning of the year as well as to focus our teaching for our classes and the entire grade. Shifting grade-wide assessments to the beginning of the year brings teachers together as we begin to plan and teach, rather than partway through or at the end of a year. Assessment then becomes part of a cycle of constructing teaching and learning rather than merely another mechanism of reporting.

See page 35 for the Performance-Based Assessment template.

Linking Formative and Summative Assessment

By *formative* we mean assessments that provide us with information about students' strengths, challenges, and progress toward our learning goal.

The PBA has become a powerful formative assessment for us. We realize, though, that one assessment can't tell us everything we need to know. While we use the PBA as an initial source of data, we need to constantly gather varied sources of information to paint a clearer picture and be more responsive teachers—if we depend on one source of information we can sometimes make false assumptions. These assessments are not used to generate marks, but are used to guide our planning for teaching. Formative assessment can be particularly powerful for students, because students receive descriptive feedback while in the process of learning and creating. It is a way to bring students into the process of their own learning.

In our classes, the PBA we use for reading nonfiction gives us a lot of information, including students' use of strategies, their comprehension skills, and their ability to analyze. We use information from the PBA to choose two or three thinking skills to focus on in our instruction. We then modify our instructional goals based on ongoing formative assessment. Weaving these goals into our units, we explicitly instruct students in these skills and ensure that our summative assessments are aligned with the goals we set and the instruction we give.

Here is an example of a planning sheet following the PBA in Mehjabeen's Grade 8 Humanities class. Building from this, she teaches and formatively assesses students on the development of these thinking skills. At the end of each unit, regardless of the theme of the unit, she assesses the thinking skills being targeted as part of the summative assessment. For example, if she is focusing on making connections in a given unit, students would have to make connections and would be assessed on them in the summative assessment.

SAMPLE PBA–PLANNING WORKSHEET

Class: Humanities 8

Strengths	Goals and Planning: I would like to see
• strong vocabulary skills • enthusiastic readers • confident • strong writers • some rudimentary note-making skills (webs and diagrams used)	• students creating their own strategies and reflecting on their success—work on metacognitive processes • students successfully distinguishing between main ideas and details • students reading between the lines • students holding their thinking, make connections between real life and subject areas

Areas to work on:
- Distinguishing between main idea and detail
- Inference
- Making connections
- Thinking about their thinking
- Connecting with big ideas

Planning Notes
- Try to work on some metacognitive processes first with some strategies that they are comfortable with, then move to inference and making connections
- Teach them to hold their thinking – use sticky notes and one graphic organizer – can we incorporate technology into this?
- How can we build on their note-making skills? Should we teach mind-mapping first and then another form in the second term?

Planning Summative Assessment

When we begin to think about the summative assessments we want our students to engage in, we try to create tasks that require them to

- connect what they already know to new information
- process ideas and information
- personalize and transform the ideas and processes we have been developing
- demonstrate their competence with the goals we've set for the unit

Often in the course of a unit we don't get to all the goals we set; we may spend more time going more deeply into one or two of those goals, building and tracking students' development. In our summative assessment (which sometimes has to be tweaked to address the goals we actually worked on) we evaluate the thinking skills we have worked on in depth together.

Some of these summative assessments mirror the PBA: students have to construct meaning from text(s), analyze, and respond. This helps us to see if the thinking skill we have been targeting has been developed and can be applied more independently. In order to keep this performance task as authentic as possible, we include strategies that support students in their work, such as talk time, planning time, graphic organizers, opportunities to discuss their interpretation of the task, and peer and teacher feedback throughout the process. There is no job that requires people to work completely independently of one another and under artificial time constraints, which is why we do not use tests. We want our classrooms to reflect our belief that working together is core to the discipline of English language arts. Readers and writers and thinkers draw from one another and we want to create a community of practitioners in our classrooms.

Other summative assessments involve a performance task that we engage in over time. The products that students typically create in ELA classrooms are complex. Mastering the form of a narrative essay, a persuasive speech, a free-verse poem, or a blog, for example, can become the performance task for a unit or lesson sequence. We let students know what the task is at the beginning of the unit and together we identify the features of the form, the processes built into the creation of the form, and the skills that we need to develop to complete the task successfully. We work through the stages together, then students have the opportunity to practice, first in groups and then independently, using the strategies that we've been working with. In this way, this second type of summative assessment becomes a frame for the unit.

For us, summative assessments are typically used at the end of an instructional sequence, once students have had the opportunity to learn and practice skills we've been working on, supported by descriptive feedback on their progress. For longer units, this means that we often have a summative assessment partway through in addition to one at the end. Students demonstrate their learning through performance tasks that require them to use the key skills we've been targeting and the concepts we've been exploring together. If we haven't taught it, we don't summatively assess it.

Considerations for Summative Assessment

While we want to provide students with choice, we need to balance that with what they need to know in order to be successful. This is particularly true for summative assessments. If we include format options that we haven't taught explicitly, we assess the thinking or organization rather than the form. For example, if we offer collage as an option for a summative assessment, but we haven't spent time teaching the features of a collage or developing criteria around what makes an effective one, we would focus our assessment on the thinking behind the collage, rather than the collage itself—the process rather than the product. Students would write an explanation of their choices and discuss how these fulfill the criteria of the task.

In a unit we co-planned on the darkness in humanity, we spent some time exploring connotation; this is another example of assessing thinking but not the form itself. One of the tasks we set for students was to choose one of five words (*darkness*, *violence*, *conflict*, *pain*, or *destruction*) and create an original image or symbol, or a collage, that defined/explained/explored the word. We also asked that they provide a brief written explanation (bullets/charts/paragraph) of the thinking behind the image. This is the rubric we used that focused solely on their thinking.

	Work that does not meet expectations will be returned; re-submit when it meets expectations.		
Image Rubric	Minimally Meets Expectations	Fully Meets Expectations	Exceeds Expectations
Understanding of word (denotation and connotation)	• image(s) convey(s) a basic understanding of the word, with some associations and examples	• image(s) convey(s) a thorough understanding of the word, with several associations and examples	• image(s) convey(s) an insightful understanding of the word, with rich multiple associations and examples

Krista had never taught her students explicitly how to make a film. She knew that if she was going to assess the form, she would need to teach them about the form itself. But how to give them formative feedback to prepare for a summative film-making task? For this unit, students created book trailers for novels. This gave Krista the chance to formatively assess the students' use of text, sound, images, transitions, and organization. Because all the students shared their trailers, they were able to gather lists of techniques and decisions they felt were particularly effective that they would try when they created a movie later in the year.

There are times when we do offer a choice of summative tasks while at the same time assessing form. Krista looked at documentaries and persuasive essays in a unit where students explored the question, "How is meaning shaped and how do we shape meaning?" During the course of the unit, students engaged in critical reading activities of documentaries, speeches, and essays. They analyzed how filmmakers use text tracks, audio tracks, and visual tracks to create meaning and to persuade viewers. They also looked at the rhetorical techniques speech and essay writers use to convince audiences of their arguments. Then they practiced writing persuasive pieces in small groups.

Krista gives students the option of writing a persuasive essay or developing a short persuasive film. They had studied both forms, they had practiced both forms with descriptive feedback, and they could choose whichever form they wanted to share their learning of how we shape meaning for particular purposes. Below are the rubrics she used. There are a few small changes (students who chose the essay were assessed on their sentence structure and word choice, while students who chose the film were assessed on their use of images and sound), but the assessment for ideas and support is identical.

SAMPLE RUBRIC FOR A PERSUASIVE ESSAY

Aspect	A good start.	You did it. An effective argument.	Wow. An elegant, convincing argument.
SNAPSHOT	*The writing is generally clear and conversational, with a beginning, middle, and end. However, development is uneven, and the writer uses a limited repertoire of language, sentences, and techniques.*	*The writing is clear and logical, with some evidence of depth or maturity. Meets the require-ments of the task with a sense of purpose and control, and with some variety in language, sentences, and techniques.*	*The writing creates an impact on the reader, with a sense of vitality and finesse. It exceeds the requirements of the task and features some complex and mature language, ideas, and techniques. Few, if any, errors.*
MEANING • ideas • support -details and examples -ethical, logical, and emotional appeals -opposing arguments	• ideas are generally straightforward and clear; unevenly developed • some relevant examples, details; may rely on general knowledge, emotion; an attempt is made to use two types of appeals (ethical, logical, emotional); opposing arguments may not be acknowledged or countered effectively	• ideas are fully developed and show depth in places • supporting details and examples are relevant and support main points; effective use of logical and emotional appeals; opposing arguments are acknowledged and countered	• ideas are fully developed with some originality, maturity, and individuality • well-chosen details and examples often show some subtlety; powerful use of ethical, logical, and emotional appeals; opposing arguments are acknowledged and countered convincingly
STYLE • sentences • word choice • rhetorical devices and persuasive techniques	• some sentence variety, mostly playing with length • straightforward vocabulary; word choice is appropriate, not concise • some evidence of deliberate techniques	• varied length and type of sentences • varied and appropriate language; some complex vocabulary • uses a variety of stylistic or rhetorical techniques	• wide repertoire of effective sentence structures that create specific effects • precise, concise language; effective, economical word choice • takes risks with a variety of techniques; shows originality, inventiveness
FORM • beginning • organization and transitions • ending	• opening introduces the topic • sequence is generally logical but may lack sense of direction; transitions awkward or missing in places	• opening establishes context and purpose, attempts to engage • sequence is logical; transitions help to connect ideas clearly	• engaging introduction • sound structure; seems effortless and natural; smooth transitions throughout

Aspect	A good start.	You did it. An effective argument.	Wow. An elegant, convincing argument.
	• conclusion may be very short or formulaic	• explicit, logical conclusion	• satisfying conclusion usually has some "punch"
CONVENTIONS • spelling • sentence structure and punctuation • usage	• includes noticeable errors that may distract the reader but do not interfere with meaning	• may include some errors; these are generally not serious and do not distract the reader	• few errors; these do not distract the reader (may only be noticeable when the reader looks for them)

Adapted from BC Performance Standards for Reading and Writing (2002)

SAMPLE RUBRIC FOR A PERSUASIVE FILM

Aspect	A good start.	You did it. An effective argument.	Wow. An elegant, convincing argument.
SNAPSHOT	*The film is generally clear, with a beginning, middle, and end. However, development is uneven, and the student uses a limited repertoire of language, ideas, and techniques.*	*The film is clear and logical, with some evidence of depth or maturity. Meets the requirements of the task with a sense of purpose and control, and with some variety in language, ideas, and techniques.*	*The film creates an impact on the reader, with a sense of vitality and finesse. It exceeds the requirements of the task, and features some complex and mature language, ideas, and techniques.*
MEANING • ideas • support -details and examples -ethical, logical, and emotional appeals -opposing arguments	• ideas are generally straightforward and clear; unevenly developed • some relevant examples, details; may rely on general knowledge, emotion; an attempt is made to use two types of appeals (ethical, logical, emotional); opposing arguments may not be acknowledged or countered effectively	• ideas are fully developed and show depth in places • supporting details and examples are relevant and support main points; effective use of logical and emotional appeals; opposing arguments are acknowledged and countered	• ideas are fully developed with some originality, maturity, and individuality • well-chosen details and examples often show some subtlety; powerful use of ethical, logical, and emotional appeals; opposing arguments are acknowledged and countered convincingly
STYLE • visual and audio tracks • rhetorical devices and persuasive techniques	• some well-chosen images and sound; some may be too literal; some don't work well together or fit the mood or tone of the piece • some evidence of deliberate techniques	• well-chosen images and sound create specific effects • uses a variety of stylistic or rhetorical techniques	• well-chosen images and sound create specific effects; some subtlety; images and sound work together to create a given mood or tone • takes risks with a variety of techniques; shows originality, inventiveness

Aspect	A good start.	You did it. An effective argument.	Wow. An elegant, convincing argument.
FORM • beginning • organization and transitions • ending	• opening introduces the topic • sequence is generally logical but may lack sense of direction; transitions awkward or missing in places • conclusion may be very short or formulaic	• opening establishes context and purpose, attempts to engage • sequence is logical; transitions help to connect ideas clearly • explicit, logical conclusion	• engaging introduction • sound structure; seems effortless and natural; smooth transitions throughout • satisfying conclusion usually has some "punch"
CONVENTIONS (for text track) • spelling • sentence structure and punctuation • usage	• includes noticeable errors that may distract the reader but do not interfere with meaning	• may include some errors; these are generally not serious and do not distract the reader	• few errors; these do not distract the reader (may only be noticeable when the reader looks for them)

*Please ensure that the sound is balanced in the film—that the music doesn't drown out the speaking, for example.
*You must include a Works Cited page (screen). Follow the guidelines in the links provided.

We want to create a classroom where students become readers, writers, and thinkers together. While we recognize that we have to report achievement using numbers or letters, we use assessment primarily to track and support their growth; in order to do this, we formatively assess to see where they are in their development and to identify how we're going to move them forward. Assessment is a tool we use first and foremost to understand what our students can do. It gives us the information we need to plan intentionally, responsively, and thoughtfully.

As we work through the development of goals for our students based on all the formative assessment, surveys, and information gathering that we do, we involve students in this process of thinking about and setting goals based on their own strengths and areas of challenge. They become part of the planning of their own learning; they assess with us whether our teaching is making a difference and help us to figure out what else it is that they need to improve. When they engage in a summative assessment, they are aware of what it is that they will be assessed on and what that would look like.

We see responsive teaching as shared ownership and authorship of assessment, planning, and learning.

Responsive Planning

Reflection and goal-setting allow us to modify our planning as we go, and remind us to be constantly aware of our students' changing abilities and needs. We have all had that experience where a unit that went so well one year falls flat the next. We can't teach the same unit to different groups of students without making necessary adaptations and expect it to work just as well.

Like many teachers in middle and secondary schools, we often teach two or three sections of the same course, and it can be tempting to teach the identical lesson to all of our students. In our exploration of how to create effective units for all learners, we have found that getting to know our students and then designing a unit with all of them in mind has a significant payoff. Rather than making multiple adaptations during the unit, we plan for diversity from the beginning; as a result, students are more engaged and have more voice and

We make significant changes year to year depending on what we learn about our students, what's going on in the world, and what new texts we encounter. Our goal is to continue to develop ways to differentiate even more between the same sections of a course in a given year, as each group of students is unique in their interests, strengths, and challenges.

See page 36 for the Getting to Know You survey form.

ownership over what they are learning and how they are learning it. When we plan with the needs of specific students in mind, we often find that we meet the needs of more students than we anticipated.

In the past we have begun the year with interest and learning surveys of our students. We used these tools to help students choose independent novels or topics for papers, among other things. We've recently moved to using them for overall planning, including adapting our plans for different sections of the same course. We don't use this information to plan entirely different units of study for each block of the same course; we do, however, make small adaptations based on the overall profile of the classes. For example, Leyton has had two very different Humanities 9 classes, one that was very focused and task-oriented, and one that was more active and artistically inclined. He encouraged one group to try a variety of forms of expression; he kept the other group focused on one type of form and worked to deepen their thinking skills.

The tools we have used to gather information about our students include

- surveys of student interests
- learning style/multiple intelligence inventories
- strengths and challenges charts
- conversations with or notes from teachers and counselors
- performance-based assessments (see page 35)
- student samples or classroom artifacts
- Getting to Know You (as people and learners) surveys (see page 36)

Once we've collected some of this information, collating it into a class profile helps us make planning decisions. This information includes samples of student work from the first unit of the year. While some of the information is similar to what we collect from the PBA, this profile is more comprehensive. It becomes an invaluable visual tool for effectively bringing together and planning from students' needs and interests.

SAMPLE CLASS PROFILE

Class Strengths	Class Stretches
• many are willing to share their thinking out loud • thoughtful • do their best thinking on a structured task in quiet • some very good writers • a lot of sensitivity, group of girls that are really connected, some have had personal tragedy and realize how they can help and support each other	• some kids that really struggle with organization and attention • making connections • determining importance • summarizing • inferencing • emotional turmoil in a lot of these kids' lives

Class Strengths	Class Stretches
• humor in the class (i.e., Riley) • more Science type kids than Fine Arts • word skills • using text features (had been working on them before the assessment) • eclectic class (faiths, home life, learning challenges) • "get it" more – they have more intellectual ability than they show in interaction • see it more in their work than in their class interactions • excellent heart maps	• need to be told what to do • supporting their ideas/understandings • can't handle chaos • these kids have not had a drama across the curriculum or multimodal classroom experience at this school yet • not really that metacognitive yet

Class Goals

- reading comprehension (making connections, determining importance)
- enjoyment of reading and learning
- engagement (almost like someone found a switch and turned them off)
- want the kids to be more independent, know what they have to do and be able to determine or develop strategies to get the job done

Decisions

- building criteria with them to help them analyze tasks and develop approaches
- need to develop their ability to show what they know in different ways
- brainstorm how they might show what they know in different ways
- commonplace book – need to give them an opportunity to make a plan, in the assessment piece have them make a plan for next wave of commonplace books
- have them make their own reading logs using criteria
- develop rubrics with them for reading logs
- lit circles will require them to make choices
- metacognitive step on the reading logs
- exit slips – what was the big idea today?– show or tell me in words, diagrams, etc.
- have them explain to a partner how they will find supporting ideas and information – don't tell them, have them figure it out – lots of think, pair, share

Adapted from Brownlie & King (2000)

Using Surveys to Guide Planning

We have used surveys that ask students about their strengths and stretches or about their interests to get a general picture of our classes. Sometimes there is a clear common interest, such as sports, that we can draw on; more often, there are several topics of interest that we can try to weave into our planning. When we use these kinds of surveys throughout the year, not just at the beginning, students are involved in planning curriculum with us.

Here is a sample survey Joanne used at the end of the first term to help determine the topic of an inquiry unit for the next term. She was teaching two sections of English 8 and wanted to find a topic of interest to both groups.

SAMPLE STUDENT SURVEY: WHAT MIGHT WE INQUIRE ABOUT NEXT IN ENGLISH 8?

Rank each inquiry question below from 1 to 5 on the following scale:

1 = no interest
2 = a little interest
3 = somewhat interested, need more info
4 = quite interested
5 = very interested, intrigued

_____ How do people reveal (or hide) their true personality?
_____ How does our culture shape our beliefs and actions?
_____ How can we create a sense of belonging in our lives?
_____ What makes a good relationship? What harms/ruins relationships?
_____ What personal qualities would make the best friend?
_____ Are people basically good or basically bad?
_____ What is the best way to prevent violence in schools?

_____ Why are gangs so magnetic?

_____ What does it mean to be mature?

_____ What makes a great leader?

_____ What does it mean to be successful?

_____ What does it mean to be well-educated?

_____ What is our responsibility to those less fortunate than us?

_____ What does it mean to tell the truth? Is it ever okay to lie?

_____ How can we improve our school?

_____ How do the stories we tell shape our lives?

_____ Why do we have so much stuff?

_____ How should we deal with human cruelty?

If this survey has given you any ideas for inquiry topics/questions, add them on below:

Student responses were compiled and shared with the students to make the process of narrowing down the topics more explicit and open. Any topics with fewer than 15 responses of 4 or 5 were eliminated.

The resulting top five choices between the two sections were determined. After some discussion of what each topic might look like as a unit (and any necessary changes to make it work), students voted on their top choice; after reviewing the votes for both blocks, the topic of Truth and Lies (number 4) came out as the winner.

TOP 5 ENGLISH 8 INQUIRY TOPICS

1. Are sports really necessary?
- May need to tweak the question: Is competition necessary?
- Can deal with sports competition, but also economic, personal, academic, etc.
2. How should we deal with human cruelty?
- Might be a little bit "big" unless we narrow the scope
- What do we mean by "cruelty"? Who is "we"?
3. How do people reveal (or hide) their true personality?
- Could relate this to psychology and our own lives as well as characters in stories/movies
4. What does it mean to tell the truth? Is it ever okay to lie?
- Might have to add to the second question: "If so, when is it okay to lie? And to what extent?"
5. What personal qualities would make the best friend?
- Again, could relate this to psychology and our own lives as well as characters in stories/movies

This is an example of working with students to choose a topic that appeals to them, and of planning from students' interests. Since this way of choosing a topic for inquiry requires some lead time, it doesn't work as well for the first unit of the year; however, as we wind down a unit there is time to choose a topic with students (which gets them excited about the next unit), and to plan and find texts to support the unit.

Providing Choice Within a Unit

Whether students or teachers choose the inquiry for a unit, students can still create a personal focus within the larger topic. In a unit on relationships, students were given the choice of focusing on dating, friends, or family relationships. With each of these topics, students chose or created five questions that they wanted to explore through a variety of texts, some of which were class texts, and some of which were specific to their topic of dating, friends, or family relationships.

We've also used text sets to allow for different learning styles and different reading levels. For example, in a unit on searching, we read multiple texts as a class, but then broke into small groups to do a poetry literature circle; students selected their groups based on the type of challenge that they wanted. The text sets for the literature circles were introduced by talking a little about the poems and asking students to consider their own comfort level with poetry and the time they had available to tackle the reading task. This allowed students to self-identify and make decisions based on their own learning style and strengths. We also know that some students have times in the year when they are so heavily involved in extracurricular activities that they may simply have less time to spend on a given task, regardless of their reading ability. Other students may choose texts that provide significant challenge for them if they feel supported by a group.

Dating Text Set
Sisterhood of the Traveling Pants by Ann Brashares
The Truth about Forever by Kathleen Odean
Guitar Highway Rose by Brigid Lowry

Friends Text Set
Catalyst by Laurie Halse Anderson
Define "Normal" by Julie Anne Peters
Max the Mighty by Rodman Philbrick
Sisterhood of the Traveling Pants by Ann Brashares
The Outsiders by S.E. Hinton

Family Text Set
Catalyst by Laurie Halse Anderson
Define "Normal" by Julie Anne Peters
Walk Two Moons by Sharon Creech
The Truth about Forever by Kathleen Odean

Focusing Instruction on Student Needs

We can group students for different mini-lessons throughout the year depending on their needs and goals they set for their own learning.

Grouping students to provide them with lessons specific to their needs is another way to differentiate both within and between classes. This works particularly well with needs that we determine through careful observation and/or specific assessments; for example, when marking a set of essays, we take notes on key areas of concern or use a class list to check off achievement in key areas. We address some of these areas of concern with the whole class if we notice that a large number of students could benefit, for example, from a mini-lesson on strong leads. We address other concerns with small groups of students who need support for specific skills.

A performance-based assessment at the beginning of the year will help us identify some student strengths and challenges, but this is just one way of gathering this information. As the year progresses, we read more of our students' work, have more conversations with them, observe them in small groups, and generally get to know them better as people and learners, and so have more information to help us plan more responsively. Every class has its own personality, strengths, and challenges. We need to remember that, within any given class profile, there will be individual students who fall outside that general description. It's important not to leave those students behind in our planning of lessons and assessments. Each summative assessment, for example, needs to be open-ended enough to allow for adaptations for students who struggle, students who need a challenge, and students who just need to do it differently, while still meeting the expected outcomes of the assessment and curriculum.

Honoring and Developing Different Ways of Learning

When it comes to designing lessons and units based on students' learning styles and strengths, we know going in that we will have a variety of students in any given class and that we should incorporate all learning styles into our teaching.

We don't need to use all styles and strengths in every lesson or activity, but over the course of the unit we need to give every student a chance to tackle that

One year Joanne had a large number of kinesthetic learners, so she consciously included activities that provided for movement in each of her classes. When she was modeling how to write the personal essay, she had her students write for a few minutes on a question. Then she had them scan their quickwrites for one idea they thought was interesting and/or important. Then they needed to get up, find someone in another group, share their ideas, and bring both ideas back to their own group to share. They had to choose two ideas they all thought should be included in the essay, and be prepared to defend their thinking. This small bit of movement made a lot of difference for her students.

big inquiry question using their preferred learning style. This is a way of honoring them as learners. At the beginning of a unit we co-planned on the theme of hope, we had students watch a talk by Steven Pinker at TED.com, share their reactions and big ideas in small groups, and work with in partners to develop a visual or dramatic response to the question, "What does hope look like?" which we shared with the class. We encouraged students to use simile and metaphor to write a descriptive paragraph on hope, focusing on sensory images: what does hope sound like, look like, feel like? We also had them do some expository writing, inviting them to define hope and to comment on each other's definitions. Students brought quotations about hope to class, and we did a graffiti activity where they moved around the room with their pens, commenting on each other's quotations and responses to those quotations. We also had them bring in a 3D object that represents hope; they could choose to bring in a picture of that object and share it with their group on a cell phone. The "object" could be a website, blog, video, or Twitter thread. These introductory activities spanned learning styles and strengths, because we wanted students to have a way into the unit using at least one of their preferred ways of learning and thinking.

We also want students to try to learn beyond their preferred way. When we invite them to play with an idea in writing, in conversation, by reflecting on their own, through drama or art or music, they might uncover perspectives or ideas that never occurred to them before—the medium can enhance the message. If a student is not artistic but is encouraged to try to capture an idea using an image or collage, that student might see connections, ask questions, or have insights that they might have missed when using a more comfortable mode of learning or expression. Working with a group of people with a range of abilities, experiences, and interests makes the classroom a place of broader and richer learning than students can ever have on their own.

For us, responsive teaching has taken on many forms. In some cases, we reorder when we teach certain units based on the interests and needs of our students. We don't throw out what we've done; we rethink when we'll do it, or change the skill focus, or make other minor adjustments in the plan. In other cases, we continue to work on the targeted thinking skill over many lessons—so students get better at that particular skill over time. For example, we begin the year focusing on visualizing; for one group of students this focus might last just a few weeks, and for others it might last the whole year. We have often found that we carry the focus on a thinking skill into the next unit, which helps students apply and adapt these skills in new situations. We might also take a favorite lesson sequence, such as persuasion techniques, and change the form (speech or essay) as well as the content or theme. In this way we can respond to students by making the content or theme fit their interests, while at the same time addressing certain curriculum needs and perhaps re-using quality units we've taught in the past.

Over time we have come to realize that our efforts to engage learners and align formative and summative assessment have little long-term impact if students do not have opportunities to own and author their learning. It is one thing for students to feel like they are welcome, yet another for students to personalize and transform the ideas and thinking strategies that that are modeled and introduced to them. Over the last several years, the four of us have developed a number of ways to help students choose a topic or subtopic for study, to choose a text from a text set, and to set and monitor learning goals for themselves. Activities that support personalized and self-regulated learning range from approaches to instruction, like inquiry teaching and self-directed learning, to including daily or weekly reflection and goal-setting activities.

The Process of Inquiry

One of the payoffs of using inquiry in our classrooms is that it requires students to approach learning deeply from the inside out. When engaged in a process of inquiry, you make connections between what you already know, believe, and have experienced in life and what others are studying, thinking, talking, and writing about.

When students engage in inquiry they are experiencing the combined skills of data collection, analysis, reflection, synthesis, and representation used by researchers. Linguists, authors, and web designers all use the process of inquiry in their work. Inquiry is authentic. We might begin the school year by asking students to become anthropologists. We share our own journals, which we call commonplace books, and model our own processes of collecting artifacts that are meaningful—these include personal items that relate to a significant aspect of what we believe, quotes and images from other texts that we believe communicate an important or powerful message and relate to our lives and, at times, issues in the larger world.

Mini-lessons within inquiry units allow us to introduce and model strategies that can be used as tools to support students in engaging in and communicating about their inquiry. We help them build thinking skills to help them engage with and process the resources they need to make these connections. There is a slight but important shift when we move from teaching students specific skills by modeling a single approach that all students mimic to asking students what other methods they think might work.

Moving to inquiry-based teaching helps us put students at the centre of their learning, where they have to construct meaning in relation to an overarching question. Students are asked to discuss how their learning relates to issues and questions that do not have single answers. To examine and investigate a question, we need to access prior knowledge by making connections between what we already know and the topic itself. Over time we expand from developing shared knowledge to examining and proposing how the questions relate to the larger landscape of society. Students might refer to sources such as articles, research reports, videos, and websites. Within a unit, sharing of information and resources is strongly encouraged; by sharing with one another, students can compare information, refine their learning, and set new goals.

Within an integrated social studies and English language arts program, Leyton and two colleagues developed the essential question: *Is Napoleon an enduring historical figure?* Students were supported to find, summarize, and compare key information related to this question. At the end of the unit students had two performance tasks to complete related to the essential question: they used the ideas and information they acquired to support a position; they chose the information they would use. Both of these tasks required students to engage in learning based on open-ended questions.

Reflection and Goal-Setting within the Inquiry Process

Ongoing reflection is a process common to all forms of inquiry. Reflection is triggered when a situation we experience puzzles or surprises us. As we try to understand and explain what we have noticed in relationship to what we think we know, we create a hypothesis. The hypothesis, or "best guess," becomes the basis for further inquiry. The process of thinking things through—examining what has happened, creating explanations, and making plans for further action—is the reflective side of the inquiry process.

Reflection triggers action. For example, we might try an intervention in a situation to test our hypothesis and observe what happens next. We might also turn to others, including expert resources, for possible explanations or suggestions about how to proceed. Reflection and action are linked as ongoing elements of the inquiry process. In our classrooms we have used a variety of approaches to help students engage in reflection; for instance, a learning journal is an important resource for tracking the changes in thinking that happen as you reflect on situations you experience in practice.

Responsive teaching includes getting students involved in assessing and monitoring their learning. This works well within inquiry units, as reflection is core to inquiry. When students set goals for themselves, make plans regarding those goals, and monitor how they are doing over time, learning becomes personalized. By engaging in an ongoing conversation with students about their goals and progress, we can develop plans to support them as they are learning. There are many different ways to continue this conversation, including conferences, informal chats, checklists, planning sheets, dialog journals, reflection logs, exit slips, and group discussions. What's key in this process is that both students and teachers are explicit about what they notice and what they are going to do.

Performance-Based Assessment

1. Predicting: What do you think this passage will be about? How do you know?

2. Summarizing: Using a web, words, diagrams, and/or drawings, show that you can identify the key ideas and details from this passage.

3. Connections : How does what you read connect with what you already know?

4. Vocabulary

Word	Definition	How I figured out its meaning
a.		
b.		
c.		
d.		
e.		

5. Making an Inference: Read between the lines to find something that you believe to be true or figured out, but that isn't actually said. Explain your reasoning.

6. Reflecting: Was this reading easy or hard to understand? How did you help yourself understand? (If this was easy, what do you do to help yourself understand something more difficult?)

Conference Sheet
Ask, after reading, the following questions:

7. When you come to a challenging word, how do you figure it out?

Word strategies:
_____ reread it
_____ sound it out
_____ look it up in the dictionary
_____ skip it
_____ ask someone
_____ try and figure out what makes sense in the sentence

Other: _____

8. If your reading does not make sense, what do you do?

Sense strategies:
_____ reread it
_____ skip it
_____ ask someone
_____ try another book
_____ make a picture in my mind
_____ make notes on what I've read
_____ make a connection between the text, self, the world, another text

Other: _____

9. What was the main idea of the whole passage that you read?

Adapted from Brownlie, Feniak & Schrellert (2006)

Getting to Know You

All about_____

Words that describe me	My favorite books/stories	Things I like to do with my friends	My favorite activities when I'm alone	My favorite activities when I'm with my family
			Very Favorite: Other Activities:	
I'm very interested in or good at…	Things I'd like you to know about me (or you need to know about me)	My hopes and dreams for myself	The easiest ways for me to show what I know	One thing I would like to get better at in school this year

Shhhhhh!!!!

My greatest fears are…

from *Student Diversity* (2006) by Brownlie, Feniak and Schnellert.

CHAPTER 4

Thinking Through Oral Language

Krista remembers meeting her in-laws for the first time. Who can't, really? Her husband-to-be had chastised her the night before for asking him to pass the salt. "You don't ask for the salt, Krista. You ask whoever is nearest the salt and pepper shaker if they would like the salt. They will say no, presumably, and then ask you if you would like it, at which point you may say 'Yes, please.' Remember this tomorrow when you meet my folks." How's that for putting one's partner at ease? She always thought she was a fairly polite person, but she lost all confidence in her manners. In what other areas was her knowledge of etiquette deficient?

Krista's husband was having a bit of fun with her, but it was too early in their relationship for her to know for sure. In hindsight, he did her a favor. She was so preoccupied with napkin placement and remembering to switch her fork from her left hand back to her right before eating her bite of ham that she forgot about being nervous about her speech. She managed to discuss topics other than the weather, and did her share of extending and sustaining the conversation. Following the meal and visit, she left hoping she had made a passable first impression. Rather than risk a slip, Krista ate her eggs without salt, and her words flowed.

Most of us want this type of experience, minus the stress about manners. We want to be able to participate effectively in conversation; we want to be considered good listeners by our friends; we want to be able to sustain dialog throughout a first date, then a fifth date, then a meal out when we are ten years into a marriage; we want to find something witty to say at a dinner party; we want to be able to argue a point coherently, without getting flustered; we want to be considered well-spoken by our colleagues; we want to be able to speak with intelligence and poise in front of a group. In order for oral interactions to be successful, we need to be aware of context and audience, and to adjust our body language, tone, and voice to suit our purposes. And we haven't even begun to talk about the words themselves.

Explicit Teaching of Oral Language

Speaking and listening are core communication skills, and while students probably spend more time speaking and listening in classrooms than they do reading or writing, teachers often spend little time teaching these skills explicitly. This needs to change.

Given that performance rubrics for oral language are less ubiquitous than they are for reading and writing, this is a perfect place to build rubrics with students, a valuable process that can later be used in other areas.

Each of us has integrated oral language in a variety of ways, emphasizing different aspects over our careers and with different classes. Still, these core understandings about oral language and teaching oral language guide us in our practice.

Our students need to be aware of the tools and techniques effective communicators use. Among other things, students need to be introduced to active listening skills; small-group discussion skills, such as how to sustain and extend a discussion and how to invite others to participate; and oral presentation skills, such as how to capture the attention of an audience, how to speak effectively in front of a group, how to use rhetorical devices, how to use key visuals to enhance oral presentations, and how to conclude strongly. We believe they need to be taught these skills with the same attention and care we give to the teaching of reading and writing. We provide structured opportunities for students to speak and listen thoughtfully and purposefully, to reflect on their strengths and weaknesses, and to set goals for improvement. We target a skill, model it, and provide space for guided practice as we move students toward independence. Oral language has its own curricular outcomes, and they need to be assessed both formatively and summatively.

Core Understandings: Oral Language

- Students need to understand why we are asking them to discuss and/or present on a given idea or text, and understand any tasks we give them for that discussion or presentation.
- We need to use what we know about our students' oral language skills to guide oral language instruction for the whole class, for small groups, and for individuals.
- We need to model and teach what good speakers do, what good listeners do, and what good discussion participants do.
- Students need to understand that what good speakers and listeners do varies with the text and the task.
- We need to support our students in developing informal and formal presentations for specific purposes and audiences, and we need to build in opportunity for choice in presentation topics.
- Students need opportunities to build meaning with others through discussion.
- We need to support students in thinking critically by asking questions, taking other perspectives, and considering bias.
- Students need to be metacognitive in their oral language practice by noting their strengths and challenges, selecting strategies, and setting goals for their speaking, listening, and participation in discussion—with our support.
- Students need lots of practice with partner talk, small-group discussions, large-group discussions, informal presentations, formal presentations, and focused listening on a variety of topics, including ones that are student-selected.
- We need to support students in transferring the oral language skills learned in the classroom to more social situations.

These understandings focus our instruction as we integrate oral language to help students process ideas, think critically about a wide range of texts, grow as writers in writing communities, and construct meaning.

Bringing Oral Language into the Classroom

Oral language involves so much more than delivering speeches. We often invite students to write to consolidate their learning. We can use partner talk for this same purpose. Students can turn to a partner to summarize what they have read in the first section of an essay before moving on to the next. They might ask a question partway through a film, or role-play a discussion between two characters in a short story. These are simple yet powerful ways to invite students to speak at points throughout lessons.

Because speaking and listening are so central to our classrooms, the risk is that we forget about the importance of addressing them. The advantage is that opportunities for critical work and frequent practice in these areas abound. There are a number of genres that we can explore that offer lots of room to practice speaking and listening skills: spoken word poetry, storytelling, drama, music, radio documentaries, interviews, and speeches, to name a few. But we don't need to include these more formal studies to increase the amount of time we spend teaching and practicing speaking and listening with our students. Almost any lesson can be tweaked to provide more time for student talk, and most lessons will benefit from this change.

Oral language is also critical for student development as readers. With a partner or in a small group, students can work through texts together, look at them critically, compare them with others, make connections—all things that can be done individually, but the discussion is much richer when there is a sharing of ideas. Students learn the value of multiple perspectives and of collaboration.

More and more we turn to podcasts, speeches, oral stories, and poems so students can *hear* texts, and we are also inviting students to create their own oral language pieces. As technology becomes more accessible, oral language is once again becoming a powerful medium, as was radio in the first half of the last century, and as oral storytelling has always been—but now, anyone can broadcast their voice to the world. We are excited to be preparing our students to take part in new opportunities to literally have their voices heard.

The Importance of Listening

Learning to listen critically involves many of the same skills that critical readers use. When students listen to texts—be they speeches, interviews, dialogs, radio ads, radio documentaries, news, lectures, gossip, confessions, or requests—they need to listen carefully. What rhetorical devices are being used and what is their impact on the message? Are interviewers challenging their guests or lobbing easy pitches? Are the guests practicing evasion techniques? Who is speaking more in a dialog? Who has the power? How do editing decisions serve to manipulate a message or tell a story? Whose voice is heard most often? What perspective is left out? Is there tension in a discussion that students can diffuse? We can structure lessons to have students practice answering these questions using various texts, to give them the time and space to rehearse the skills that they can use in their own lives, and that can be transferred to their reading and viewing—primarily of nonfiction texts, but also of fiction texts.

Fundamental to all of this work is that students learn how important it is to listen with care to one another. When students are delivering more formal presentations, we might ask students in the audience to listen for the main idea, if that is a skill we've been working on. If all students are presenting something that answers a common inquiry question, students can take notes about ideas presented that offer interesting perspectives, ones they might draw from for an end-of-unit reflection or essay. In this way, student presentations become important and valued texts for our classes. Listening in informal discussions is something we model extensively, and we debrief throughout the year how listening behaviors are key to ensuring that everyone feels comfortable enough to take risks and that ideas don't get lost, but rather are considered and connected with others. Respect for people and ideas are core principles in all aspects of English language arts, but they are highly visible in our work with oral language.

Discussing to Make Meaning

In partners and small groups, students can construct meaning together. One of our favorite ways to begin the year is by asking big questions that relate to our opening unit or our year's theme. In a unit on happiness, we ask, "Is happiness a decision?" and following a short independent write, use the four-corners technique to divide the class into small groups. Students agree, somewhat agree, somewhat disagree, or disagree. They meet with like-minded peers, share ideas and arguments, and then move to a class debate. Sometimes the students are so engaged that we continue the discussion until the end of the period. On days two and three we read three texts on happiness, and on day four students write an impromptu piece. The debate on the first day is as important a text for this piece as are the short story, essay, and children's story we look at—not to mention being a more exciting start to the year than a line-by-line reading of the course outline. We use this impromptu piece as our diagnostic essay, rather than having students write cold on a topic in order to get a writing sample—a diagnostic that doesn't mirror the writing process.

Writing tasks are no longer kept artificially independent. Students, even in test situations, have the opportunity to discuss topics because we value the sharing that happens and know that this enriches and extends students' thinking, resulting in more powerful writing. Some students struggle to find ideas. They might start with two, but leave a discussion with four or five to include in a piece of writing. Others struggle with coherence, and having to articulate their ideas to a partner helps them to clarify their thoughts in their heads. Their subsequent writing is clearer as a result. The partner might ask questions, point out lapses in argument, suggest places where more details could be added to an outline—all through a conversation prior to writing. Some students might leave with an idea for a fresh approach or a different form.

Speaking and listening are central to the writer's workshop approach to writing instruction, as well. Low-risk activities are easy to integrate into lessons; they allow for student voice and provide a stepping stone to more daunting activities. Rather than having students share whole paragraphs or poems with one another right away, we might begin the year by asking students to share what they wrote during a quickwrite. Everyone speaks, and students benefit from hearing the multiple approaches their peers take to a given topic. Eventually students receive instruction and structured practice in how to critique effectively and respectfully, skills that will serve them well in their writing groups, as well as in innumerable social situations. Peer editing structures often involve one student reading his or her piece aloud to the group and then listening as other students offer comments. Many students have never heard their writing aloud before, and this gives them excellent insight into their own work. They discover, in this group structure, one of the most effective revision tools, one that they can use on their own: reading one's work aloud.

We continue to seek ways to make stronger links between spoken language, written language, visual communication, and all the permutations thereof. More and more we employ discussion as a text in our classrooms; we focus on teaching and assessing discussion because we value oral language as a way of making, sharing, and extending meaning.

Oral language supports both reading and writing. Most importantly, it supports thinking. It underscores the importance of working together to generate ideas and texts, and to understand and explore increasingly complex ideas and texts. In the examples that follow, we outline units that encourage students to grow as speakers and listeners. We emphasize partner talk and small-group work, structures that are at the core of most of our lessons. The more our students are asked to speak, the more instruction and practice they're given, the more likely they are to be successful at school, in the workplace, and in social situations—even at those awkward first meals with the in-laws.

Examples From our Classrooms

In Mehjabeen's senior English classes, students are provided with a variety of opportunities to analyze, create, and respond to oral texts. The first example is a mini-unit in which students engage with a series of speeches to develop an understanding of the features and impact of oral texts. Following that are some suggestions for building student response into "oral presentations" in ways that develop the skills of the audience as well as of the presenters. Then, Krista and Joanne outline their adaptation of the literature circle structure, one that is particularly effective when using short pieces of text such as poems, articles, essays, short stories, websites, and blog entries. Finally Krista shares some work she did with Tracy Sullivan on spoken-word poetry.

Famous Speeches

In English classrooms, students analyze a variety of texts, including essays, fiction, nonfiction, poetry, drama, and art. In the mini-unit presented here, students work through the analysis of famous speeches. Because speeches are oral texts, Mehjabeen designs the unit so that students engage with the texts in ways that foreground the features of oral language. Rather than analyze speeches as oral texts recorded on paper, Mehjabeen begins the unit by having students immerse themselves in the experience of oral language, in speaking and listening. The assessment for the unit is also based on oral texts that students produce: at the end of the unit students are not assessed in the form of a written essay or exam about the speeches in the unit; rather, they are asked to create oral texts.

Each of the speeches in this unit has immediate impact on students as they appeal to strong themes such as hope and despair, difference, and common humanity. They also reference key events in history, such as those of September 11, 2001; the Holocaust; the American Civil Rights movement; and Indian independence from Britain.

Depending on when she is teaching this unit, Mehjabeen will often replace one of the speeches with a more current speech, such as an inaugural address, a speech by an important Canadian figure such as the Governor General or Prime Minister, or a more current Nobel lecture. She always uses some of the speeches listed, as they are ones that have continued to inspire her and others for years.

UNIT THEME
Finding hope within conflict and despair

UNIT OBJECTIVES
• Students will develop an understanding of the features and techniques of oral language as well as of its effects and impact on individuals and society.

- Students will become skilled and responsive listeners and skilled and creative users of oral language.

See page 50 for Four Quadrants Graphic Organizer.

ENDURING UNDERSTANDINGS FOR UNIT

1. Hope emerges from conflict and struggle.
2. By appealing to what is most important to people (our values), we can find ways to reach across and build on our differences.
3. The language we use can both obfuscate/hide and clarify what we understand to be true.
4. The language we use reveals our beliefs and values, can be used to create and sustain hope, and can separate us from or unite us with others.

ASSESSMENT

- Formative: group analysis, choral readings
- Summative: group readers theater performance text, individual speech

TEXT SET

"2001 Nobel Lecture" by Kofi Anaan
"The Perils of Indifference" by Elie Wiesel
"I Have a Dream" by Martin Luther King, Jr.
"A More Perfect Union" or "Inaugural Address" by Barack Obama
"1993 Nobel Lecture" by Toni Morrison
"Speech On the Granting of Indian Independence" by Jawaharlal Nehru

Lesson 1: Listening to a Speech—imagery and emotional impact

- Mehjabeen begins the unit by having her students listen to one of the speeches. In this lesson, she reads the speech out to the class. The intention behind this approach is to have students "experience" an oral text as an oral text, rather than as a written text.
- As she reads, students are asked to record ideas in the Four Quadrants Graphic Organizer (see page 50). We find that many of our students have not had the experience of listening to a formal speech and the Four Quadrants can help to focus their listening if they need it. More often, however, we find that students become "caught up" in the listening and forget to write anything down. As the intention of the unit is to engage students in the experience of oral language, this kind of student response is welcome.
- Once she has completed the reading, Mehjabeen asks students to share the dominant images in their minds after hearing the speech. She then continues to debrief the reading by having them identify the emotions they felt and the words/phrases that had an impact on them.
- Mehjabeen's next step is to have students look up any vocabulary that they are unfamiliar with. Sometimes, if she has a class that struggles with vocabulary, she will provide them with a vocabulary exercise prior to the reading of the speech or immediately following the first class. One example of such an exercise is the creation of a concept map from some of the key words in the speech. This kind of complex vocabulary exploration develops a deep understanding of the concepts of the speech, as it forces students to make connections between words rather than simply look up their meaning. Once students have completed the concept map, they have already developed a strong understanding of some of the key messages and themes of the speech itself.

Lesson 2: Recitation—getting inside the sounds

While it may seem that the logical next step in the unit would be to analyze the speech for techniques and theme, Mehjabeen does not move too quickly to that step. Instead, she continues to immerse students in the oral nature of the text.

- Using the same speech from the class before, Mehjabeen divides her class into groups, divides the speech into sections, and gives each group one section. (At this point, she provides them with a written copy of the speech that they can read and write on.)
- Keeping the first section for herself, Mehjabeen models how to read the section aloud. She models a variety of oral reading styles/techniques and has students practice them with her. Students are then asked to work in their groups with their own section, practicing these various styles/techniques.
  - One person reads each sentence slowly and the others repeat the sentence as she finishes.
  - The whole group reads the section together.
  - One person reads one sentence, the next person reads another, the next person continues with the next sentence; this is repeated until the section has been read three times.
  - Call and answer: One person reads and looks at a person who repeats, the person who has repeated then reads the next sentence and looks at another who then repeats; the pattern continues.
  - Everyone goes outside or to an enclosed space with sound protection and yells their section at the same time.
- Many of the speeches that Mehjabeen uses are available in audio or video format and it is at this point in the lesson sequence that she will have students listen to or watch the speech. By waiting until students have recited and heard the speech a few times and have explored the vocabulary, she makes the impact of listening or watching much greater.

Lesson 3: Rhetorical Analysis – modeling and think-aloud

In the third lesson, Mehjabeen begins the analysis of the text with her students. In order to demonstrate how their experience of reciting the speech aloud has influenced their understanding, Mehjabeen grounds this analysis in another read-aloud, this time with a different emphasis.

- Mehjabeen copies the speech onto an overhead transparency and models for students how to build from the Four Quadrants that they completed during the first lesson. Students are provided with the following techniques (written on strips of paper and placed in a envelope on their tables):

Use of Anecdote	Appeal to Emotion (pathos)
Personal Connections	Appeal to Reason/Logic
Metaphor	Appeal to Ethics (sense of right and wrong)
Rhetorical Questioning	Imagery
Theme	Concrete Examples
Motif	Direct Address/Audience
Allusions to Other Well-known Texts	

- As Mehjabeen reads through the speech once more, students are asked to identify examples of the techniques in the speech. As she or the students notice these techniques, she marks them on the overhead transparency. Students mark their own speeches with these techniques. What is important in this process is that, although students are working with a written copy of the speech, they continue to experience the impact of the techniques by listening rather than by reading. This approach forces them to continue to make meaning with a text in its oral rather than written form.
- Once this initial analysis is complete, Mehjabeen leads the class in a discussion about the themes of the text. This is the first time since the beginning of the unit that the class is discussing the "meaning" of the text. By this point, however, students are generally able to identify the most significant themes and can easily ground them in examples and techniques from the speech itself.
- Students are then asked to work in groups to identify the most significant technique in their section, and to explain how and why it contributes to the meaning of the entire text.

Lesson 4: Group Analysis

- Mehjabeen selects a second speech and has students work through its analysis. While she does not have the class re-do the Four Quadrants or the group recitations, she does have them go through the entire rhetorical analysis. She reads out the speech, and students in their groups identify the techniques, imagery, and significant vocabulary. As a class, they discuss the various themes and techniques and compare them to the first speech.
- At this point in the unit, Mehjabeen might select a third speech to analyze as a class, or she might provide each of the groups with a speech to analyze on their own. Either way, it is important for students to tackle at least three whole speeches.

Lesson 5: Readers Theater—playing with theme and technique

Shifting back to recitation, Mehjabeen has her students create a performance text out of the speeches.

- She asks them to pull together passages from the three speeches to create a performance. The organization of the performance does not have to be based in the logic of the texts, but rather should be a "creation" of the students, and can be organized around technique, theme, imagery, ideas, or contrasts.
- With the class, Mehjabeen develops criteria for an engaging readers theater performance. See page 51 for an example of the instructions and the rubric created with one of her English 11 classes.
- Students perform their texts in front of each other. Each group selects one other group and provides them with feedback (in addition to the teacher's feedback) on their performance using the criteria.
- If students find that they are not satisfied with their performance, they are able to redo the performance and to choose another group to assess them, once they have thought through and incorporated the feedback from the first group.

See page 51 for Readers Theater instructions and rubric.

Lesson 6: Writing Speeches—based on theme

The final assignment for this unit is for students to write their own speeches.

- The topic for student speeches emerges from the speeches they have analyzed. In this final assignment, students can either choose a quote from one of the speeches to explore in detail in their own speech, or they can select a theme that is common to all of them such as "common humanity," "indifference to suffering," "hope," etc. In their speeches, students are required to incorporate at least three rhetorical techniques that they have identified in the other speeches.
- Students are assessed only on their oral presentation of their speech, not on their written text, and the assessment includes their ability to have impact using their voice and expression.

Responding to Oral Presentations

In the speech unit, one factor that has significant impact on student learning is that the very nature of oral language requires an audience. As a result, students are engaged with each other as they both recite and listen. The audience is not passive. In order to ensure that students are never passive audiences when they are listening to each other present, Mehjabeen tries to build in an audience response technique whenever possible.

Example 1: Responding and Reflecting

In Mehjabeen's Grade 11 English class, one of the summative assessments for her second-term unit is a multimedia presentation. In the presentations, students are assessed on their ability to create and develop an argument using the techniques of multimedia. The thesis of the presentation draws from the ideas/texts of the larger thematic unit that the class is exploring.

In their response, the students in the audience are asked to identify the impact of the presentation on them, as well as if and how the presentation accomplished its goal of convincing them of its thesis. Students are asked to identify the thesis, the most powerful ideas and language in the presentation, and its impact on them (see Audience Response on page 52). They are then asked to write a reflection on each of the presentations. At the end of the presentations, students write an in-class essay on one of the themes emerging from the presentations. By both creating and responding to these presentations, students develop a deep understanding of the effective use of multimedia, its conventions and techniques.

See page 52 for Audience Response form.

Example 2: Peer Assessment

Oral presentations are a skill that Mehjabeen works on with her class throughout the year. Each time students do a presentation, they receive feedback from their peers on how they did and how they can improve. Each presenter receives feedback from four students in the class, selected at random. Referencing the Rubric for Oral Presentations on page 54, the students providing feedback complete the Student Feedback on Oral Presentations sheet (page 53) following the

See page 53 for Student Feedback on Oral Presentations sheet; see page 54 for Rubric for Oral Presentations.

presentation. For #4 on the feedback sheet, the presenters are asked to identify a specific area that they would like to receive feedback on.

Example 3: Blogging

In Mehjabeen's Grade 12 English class, students present a poem orally and lead the analysis of that poem for the class. Students in the audience are asked to write an essay on one or two of the poems presented, incorporating ideas from the presentation. They are also asked to contribute positive critique on the presentation in a class blog. They have to post at least twice during the cycle of presentations, and their postings have to engage in a thoughtful and positive manner. Below are some postings from the class blog in response to the poems and presentations:

> "I like that you talked about two poems, it helped to see more than one example of his writing. Even though I wasn't a fan of the second poem you were very clear in your explanations and I was able to understand the poem."

> "I thought that Kelly and Nancy's [not the students' real names] choice of 'The Hollow Men' was a very good one. The poem was complex and thought provoking, and it had a lot of depth and detail. I also liked the way they went around to each group explaining the poem and answering questions, and later went over the whole poem as a group."

> "I thought that Nancy and Kelly made a good choice by reading it to us and telling us to close our eyes. This way I was able to concentrate strictly on the image. It was a great demonstration of free verse. Clearly I really enjoyed this poem particularly the way he writes repetition of meaning not only repetition of exact phrases such as 'The eyes are not here, There are no eyes here.' It was very interesting so thanks for sharing this poem."

> "The way you three presented this poem was hands-down the greatest presentation so far. The entire class was fairly involved in good amount; we'd be in discussion for 5 minutes, and then introspection for 5, and back to discussion. It really helped bring about analysis/understanding. Personally I disagreed with the meanings many people retrieved from Sandberg's poetry but I felt that meaning I received from it was further deepened by the opposition! The poem has great FEELING to it, that I personally loved due to the fact I don't really belong in suburbs. I felt Sandberg's depiction of the reality of Chicago was great, and further enhanced by the contrast the class found."

> "The way you presented the poem was perfect. You read it very well and the power point presentation was interesting and funny. I realized that I enjoy free verse and Walt Whitman's style of writing. He writes in a way that he captures a quick moment with intensity and clarity and challenges the definition of prose and poetry."

Poetry Literature Circles

In addition to studying oral texts, creating oral texts, and responding to them, we all focus on developing discussion skills with our students, so literature circles make frequent appearances in our classrooms. We began using literature circles with novels, and this remains an important practice for us, but we have also found it to be a powerful structure to use with shorter texts. Krista and Joanne often organize literature circles for poetry.

We find that doing this type of literature circle, with an emphasis on discussion skills, has a positive impact on future discussion in our classrooms. We work to make the many layers of a good discussion more apparent. Students become aware of the complexity of effective discussions, and of the skills needed to speak, listen, and learn in small groups.

Lesson 1: Fishbowl

See page 55 for Literature Circles Instruction Sheet.

We like to begin with a "fishbowl" with several other staff members in which we model a discussion of a shared text for students. We aim for five adults, including teachers with prep blocks, administrators, the librarian, counselors, and any other staff members who may be available and willing. If we are doing this with multiple blocks, we like to choose a different text for each block so the discussions are fresh. To prepare, we ask that our fishbowl discussion participants read and mark the text we provide for them, using the same sheet of instructions we give the students (see Literature Circles Instruction Sheet on page 55).

We begin the class by giving the students a copy of the adults' text to skim, and the discussion rubric. Or, we have students generate criteria for a good discussion after watching the fishbowl. We explain briefly how the literature circles will work—that for the next three classes, their homework will be to mark the text their group chose for discussion. The classes themselves will begin with small-group discussions of the selected texts, followed by a metacognitive exercise (a discussion of their discussion) that will help them complete their self-evaluations, followed by time to write their response. We then introduce the adult volunteers and ask them to show the students their marked texts and talk a bit about their process. The last thing we do before initiating the discussion is to have the students read over the rubric. Students sit in groups and we assign each group an adult to evaluate according to the criteria on the rubric.

Following a 20-minute discussion of the text comes the most interesting part of the process: a five-minute discussion of the discussion. We talk about what worked, what question elicited the most interesting response, our surprises with the direction of the discussion, our favorite threads, and so on. Following this, we turn to the students for their evaluations of our participation.

After thanking the participants, we use the remainder of the class to prepare students for the literature circles to follow. We review the instruction sheets; then we introduce the text sets, all of which touch in some way on the theme of the unit. We typically gather five sets of four texts at different levels of challenge, according to our students' needs. We introduce them not by referring to their difficulty level, but by highlighting one or two texts in each set, and noting how much time and experience with the given genre each set might require. Students have about five minutes to choose a package of texts, meet briefly with their resulting group, and decide on the text they will use for their first discussion. For homework, students read and mark the text using one color of ink; during

POETRY TEXT SETS FOR A GRADE 12 UNIT ON STORY

Set #1 (easiest)
"Last Ride" by Andrea Holtslander
"Canada: Case History" by Earle Birney
"Sign for My Father, Who Stressed the Bunt" by David Bottoms
"Picketing Supermarkets" by Tom Wayman

Set #2 (middle)
"Warren Pryor" by Alden Nowlan
"A Poem on the Underground Wall" by Paul Simon
"what she was wearing" by Denver Butson
"Sadie and Maud" by Gwendolyn Brooks

Set #3 (middle)
"The Unknown Citizen" by W.H. Auden
"puce fairy book" by Alice Major
"Advice to the Young" by Miriam Waddington
"anyone lived in a pretty how town" by e.e. cummings

Set #4 (middle–challenging)
"A Brave and Startling Truth" by Maya Angelou
"'Out, Out – '" by Robert Frost
"My Last Duchess" by Robert Browning
"To You Who Would Wage War Against Me" by Kateri Akiwenzie Damm

Set #5 (challenging)
"Dover Beach" by Matthew Arnold
"This Is a Photograph of Me" by Margaret Atwood
"Auto Wreck" by Karl Shapiro
"All the world's a stage" from *As You Like It* by William Shakespeare

their discussions, they will use another color to record their thinking and ideas. This helps us in our final evaluation as we can see the thinking they do before and during the discussion.

Lesson 2: Literature Circle #1

After a quick review of the structure of the day (discussion, metadiscussion, self-evaluation, reflection/response), students begin their discussions, making notes on the text as they go. While students discuss in their groups, we move from group to group, observing and taking notes. When we do this with younger students, we find that it is helpful to have an adult facilitate the first one or two discussions. This sometimes means that not all of the discussions can take place at the same time; students who are not discussing are given a different task. The goal is to move students to independence, but we move more slowly or faster depending on the abilities of our students.

Following the students' metadiscussions, we debrief what they feel are their strengths and weaknesses. As a class, we brainstorm strategies for drawing out quieter people, in part by highlighting some of the nonverbal cues often associated with someone wanting to jump into a conversation (leaning forward, moving his or her pen forward, sitting up straight, starting a sentence). We debrief effective strategies for moving the discussion forward in engaging ways. We also suggest that more dominant participants practice "three before me" during the second discussion, or at least modify that to "two before me" for smaller groups. Students then set individual goals for the next discussion.

See page 57 for Group Discussion Progress Record; see page 56 for Group Discussion Rubric.

After this large-group discussion, students complete the first column of their Group Discussion Progress Record (page 57). We remind them to select the text for the second discussion, and they have the remainder of the class to complete their reflection and to begin marking the second text.

Lessons 3 and 4: Lit Circles Continue

The next class, we continue to circulate and complete observation records. This allows us to intervene and support discussion when needed. It also gives us data to consider when assigning the final summative grade for the students' small-group discussions. Following the third discussion, students highlight the words on the rubric that they feel best describe their performance for that last discussion. In addition, we collect their text sets so we can see their preparation, their reflections, and their progress records. If we disagree with students' self-assessments, we have a conference with them. Having observation records as well as their work in front of us during these conferences makes the discussion more meaningful.

Spoken Word

Krista's inspiration for this series of lessons came from a mini-unit Tracy Sullivan prepared on her practicum on spoken word.

Krista works with spoken-word poetry well into a unit on story, after her students have looked at a number of short stories, participated in poetry literature circles using poems relating to the theme, and practiced writing literary analysis paragraphs and essays. She wants to offer them a place to practice their style before moving into the last section of the unit, where students wrote personal narratives. The spoken-word poems offer students a chance to tell the same story they will tell in their personal narratives using a different form, or to tell a different story altogether.

Lesson 1: Background and Examples

Following a short history lesson on the Beat Generation, Krista shares a number of examples of spoken words, some professionally recorded, some written by former students. (Many excellent examples can be downloaded from the Internet.) Next, she and her students begin to tease out criteria (repetition, internal rhyme, pacing, sound devices, imagery, etc.)

Lesson 2: Formative Task

In order to practice the form, to give students the opportunity to interact further with one of the stories they have already read, and to review all of the stories in anticipation of the upcoming short story analysis essay, Krista invites them, in small groups, to write a spoken word from the perspective of a character from any of the stories they looked at together.

Students are assessed summatively on their interpretive reading (the content of their spoken words), as they have already been working on analysis and have had formative feedback throughout the unit; they are assessed formatively on the form, style, and presentation, since it is their first attempt. These spoken words are a lot of fun, and students are able to identify what goes into a successful one. This helps students as they begin writing their own spoken words, using their own perspective about stories that are meaningful to them.

Lesson 3: Drafting

Students have written about our love affair with celebrities, babysitting experiences, the shortcomings of language and naming, searching for a job, the stories read as a child, the pine beetle, and the probable apathy the audience will have toward the poet's effort. One student wrote a memorable parody of Ginsberg's "Howl" entitled "Towel."

See page 58 for Spoken Word Rubric.

Students begin to brainstorm topics. Their spoken words can be about anything; they simply need to think about a story they want to tell. Krista provides time to draft in class so that she can conference with students who want feedback, and so that students can engage in peer revision. Once students have drafts to work with, Krista leads the students through a whole-class revision, similar to the process outlined in chapter 5, using the list of criteria students identified in Lesson 1.

Lesson 4: Poetry Café

This is a favorite time. Some students are more nervous than they've ever been in English class—performing a spoken word is different from delivering more traditional oral presentations. But all of Krista's students present poems live, save one or two who tape theirs and play them for her after class. The audience is appreciative, often moved and surprised, and always respectful. A whole class listening to stories crafted by students and shared aloud—what could be better?

Four Quadrants Graphic Organizer

Images	Emotions

Words that have an impact on you (that you remember)	Words that you do not understand

Adapted from Brownlie & Close (1992)

Readers Theater

We are going to create a Readers Theater performance, which is essentially a dramatic reading of a text or texts. The texts you will be using are the speeches that we have been working with in this unit.

Pick a few passages from the speeches and combine them with your own thinking to create a performance. You can organize the performance around the language, a theme, an image, or an idea, or by contrasting the different texts. Be creative. Be weird. Be dramatic. **The performance does not have to make logical sense but it has to make dramatic sense—which means it has to flow or work together.**

You can work with a partner or in a group (up to four). You can use props or music, or not.

Marking Rubric

/15	1 – Snore	3 – Uh Huh	5 – Oh, yeah!
Selection of Passages • Thoughtfulness of selections • Coolness of selections (imagery, vocab, meaning)	Passages seem to be selected at random; little imagery, interesting vocab, or ideas evident.	Passages have some interesting imagery, vocab, or ideas.	Passages have very interesting imagery, vocab, or ideas. Students have really chosen the best passages from their speeches.
Construction of Performance/ Organization of Selections • Use of contrast/ juxtaposition, theme or other effect	Selections appear to be put together at random; little thought or effects are evident.	Selections are put together with some thought using a theme or an effect.	Selections are thoughtfully organized for the most impact using an effect or theme.
Performance • Voice and Tone • Expression • Timing and rehearsal • Impact on audience	• Hard to hear • Students are mostly reading; Little expression • Not well-rehearsed • Little impact on audience	• Voices are clear • May be some reading; Some expression • Rehearsed • Audience can follow	• Voices are able to really get into the language and vary the voice and tone for effect • Reading does not interfere with delivery • Well-rehearsed • Audience is engaged

Audience Response

As students present over the next couple of weeks, you, as the audience, should be taking notes on the presentations. I have provided you with an organizer below to complete during and after the presentations.

For each presentation, you are responsible for a reflection of about one page (double-spaced) typed (about 300 words).

After the last presentation, I will provide you with some topics (from the presentations) and you will write an in-class essay on one of the topics.

Guidelines for Reflection

State the thesis of the presentation; *and*

Comment on what whether you agree or disagree with the thesis; *or*

Discuss other ideas the presentation makes you think about; *or*

Discuss your reaction to the ideas of the presentation; *or*

Discuss how the presentation relates to or adds insight to the broader theme; *or*

Discuss the techniques that the presenters use to argue their thesis; *or …?*

Presenters	Thoughts, Ideas, Questions, Interesting Facts, etc.	
	Main idea/thesis: Images/key words that jumped out: Feelings/reactions/ emotions: Insights (the deep stuff) or "a-ha!" moments:	

Student Feedback on Oral Presentations

As you listen to the presenter, please complete the following (reference the rubric for the criteria):

1. One idea that stayed with you:

2. One positive comment:

3. One area/suggestion for improvement:

4. Feedback on a specific area that the presenters would like you to pay attention to:

Rubric for Oral Presentations

Aspect	D	C	B	A
The Reader and the Text	The student is unable to offer a logical interpretation of literary works that feature complex ideas and language. Often presentation is very short, with little evidence or development, and may misinterpret key features of the text. Appears to struggle to understand the text, with little success.	The student offers a narrow or superficial interpretation of literary works that feature complex ideas and language. Focuses on retelling, with limited analysis and evidence. Responses tend to be broad, undeveloped generalizations. The student is focused on understanding the text.	The student offers a logical interpretation of literary works that feature complex ideas and language. Goes beyond retelling to offer analysis and well-developed connections. The student appears to interact with the text confidently.	The student offers an analytic, thorough interpretation of works that feature complex ideas and language. Work is insightful, often speculative, and may take risks to include unusual interpretations and connections. The student appears to be engaged by the text.
Meaning • ideas and connections • literary techniques (e.g., figurative language; irony) • elements (e.g., setting, mood) • use of quotations; text references	• ideas and connections are not developed • may recognize some simple literary techniques • attempts to summarize, but misinterprets key elements • unable to provide evidence or offer relevant references to the text	• ideas and connections are generally straightforward and clear; unevenly developed • recognizes basic literary techniques • focuses on retelling, showing basic and often superficial understanding of elements and key features • references to the text are vague, not convincing	• ideas and connections are fully developed and show depth • recognizes and deals confidently with a variety of literary techniques • logically describes and analyzes elements and key features; goes beyond retelling • provides appropriate quotations and other text references as evidence	• ideas and connections are fully developed with some originality, maturity, and individuality • interprets and evaluates a variety of literary techniques • thoroughly describes and analyzes elements and key features, dealing with subtleties and nuance • chooses and integrates quotations and other text references effectively
Oral Presentation • organization • clarity • audience engagement • preparation and practice • use of visuals and media	• presentation is not organized • presentation is difficult to follow • audience is not engaged, presenters are not addressing audience • little preparation or practice is evident, presenters stumble and consult each other often • visuals and media do little to support points, may be distracting or go on for too long	• there is a beginning, middle, and end • presentation is somewhat clear, parts may be hard to follow • audience is being polite, may not be engaged • presenters pause often, have to consult notes to explain points, could use more practice • visuals and media are used, are related to content	• introduction is clear and sets up the presentation, middle is developed, and conclusion attempts to provide closure • presentation is clear • audience is paying attention, can follow the presentation • presenters are prepared • visuals and media are related to the meaning, help to make presenters' point	• introduction is engaging, middle is well-developed and supported, ending provides a "so what" • presentation is clear and well-articulated • audience is engaged, presenters have made contact and held attention with body language, eye contact, and direct speech • presenters are prepared and know their "stuff" • visuals and media enhance meaning – well-chosen

Adapted from BC Reading and Writing Performance Standards (2002)

Literature Circles Instruction Sheet

You will be working with a small group to read, discuss, and reflect on a set of texts. There are several different sets of texts; choose the set that most appeals to you. Then, form a group by finding the others who have chosen the same set of texts. Once in your group, follow the framework below.

Before the Lit Circle: Preparation

1. As a group, choose *one* of the texts to read for the discussion.
2. On your own, read the text and make notes on the page (the text set is yours to write on and keep). Comment, make connections, ask questions, note literary devices, etc. Use one color of ink for these notes, and another color for notes made during the discussion.
3. On the bottom or back of the text, write a reflection on the text (a short paragraph will do).

During the Lit Circle: Discussion

1. When you get together in your group to discuss the text you chose, begin with the Say Something strategy. Then let your discussion flow. Use your notes on the text, and your reflection to guide your discussion and/or provide new directions. Take notes during the discussion for use in later work (use a different color of ink)
2. During your discussion, focus on using and improving the discussion skills on the rubric that you have been given. At the end of the discussion, you will have about 5 minutes to talk about how the discussion went and if you met the expectations of the criteria sheet. You may wish to take notes.
3. Fill in the Discussion Skills Criteria sheet for today's discussion. Be as specific as you can and provide examples of how you did (or didn't!) meet the criteria. The first two times you do this will be for formative assessment, and you are expected to notice your areas of challenge and improve on them.

After the Lit Circle: Reflection

On your own, write a reflection on one (or more, as is appropriate) of the following questions, based on your reading and discussion of the text:

1. Have your original ideas changed? How? Why?
2. Have you seen the text from other perspectives? What are they?
3. Has your first response been confirmed? How?
4. What has been revealed to you about your classmates or yourself?

Reflection questions adapted from Probst (2004)

Group Discussion Rubric

Criteria Aspect	Not Yet Meeting	Minimally Meeting	Fully Meeting	Exceeding
Prepares to engage in the class: has read, commented, and reflected on the text	Has read text but not made any notes	Has read text and made some notes; reflection is minimal	Has read text more than once, made notes on most questions and aspects, reflected	Has read text more than once, made thorough notes and written a thoughtful reflection
Listens attentively to offerings of others; attempts to build upon and extend the thoughts of others	Gives little attention to others' ideas; does not add to ideas of others; makes a comment and withdraws	May sometimes misunderstand others' ideas; occasionally builds on others' ideas	Grasps others' ideas and attempts to connect own ideas to them and add to them	Successfully and thoughtfully builds on others' ideas with connections and extensions
Is a responsible group member: helps to draw others into discussion; refrains from sarcasm or insults; tolerates attempts of others to explore and take risks	May cut off others' ideas or may put them down; is unwilling to allow others to attempt to explore and take risks	Does not discourage others from speaking; may be occasionally and mildly sarcastic; does not discourage or encourage attempts to explore/take risks	Encourages and is respectful of others' ideas; encourages attempts to explore and take risks	Invites all voices; always respectful of others' ideas; invites and encourages attempts to explore and take risks
Is willing to probe and question, to speculate, and to take risks during the discussion	Does not go beyond basic ideas and surface questions or interpretations	Makes some attempt to go beyond surface ideas with questions or speculations	Attempts to ask some probing questions and take risks in discussion	Asks several probing questions and takes several risks with ideas in discussion
Uses appropriate methods to work toward task completion: contributes to discussion, refers to pre-discussion notes, raises questions, makes connections, summarizes thinking	Contributes infrequently or inappropriately to discussion; dominates the discussion; is not focused on task completion	Contributes to discussion but may dominate; tends to repeatedly use one or two methods to contribute to the discussion; some focus on the task	Contributes often to discussion but doesn't dominate; uses several methods to contribute to the discussion; maintains focus on completing the group task	Contributes in a balanced way to the discussion; uses a wide variety of effective methods to contribute to the discussion and to task completion

Adapted from Probst (2004)

Group Discussion Progress Record

Use this rubric to record your progress in each of the areas described below. The first two lit circles will be formatively assessed; the assessment of the last one will be summative. When you complete your self-evaluation, you must also hand in this record sheet as well as your set of texts and any notes you have made on them.

Criteria	Lit Circle #1 (F)	Lit Circle #2 (F)	Lit Circle #3 (S)
Prepares to engage in the class: has read, commented, and reflected on the text			
Listens attentively to offerings of others; attempts to build upon and extend the thoughts of others			
Is a responsible group member: helps to draw others into discussion; refrains from sarcasm or insults; tolerates and encourages attempts of others to explore and take risks			
Is willing to probe and question, to speculate, and to take risks during the discussion			
Uses appropriate methods to work toward task completion: contributes to discussion, refers to pre-discussion notes, raises questions, makes connections, summarizes thinking			
Set a specific goal for the next discussion			

Spoken Word Rubric

	Not Yet Within Expectations D	Meets Expectations (Minimal Level) C	Fully Meets Expectations B	Exceeds Expectations A
Snapshot	*Creates a work with little sense of purpose; few attempts to use poetic language*	*Attempts to develop a poetic statement with some figurative language and sound devices*	*Creates a thoughtful poetic statement that features some effective language play and imagery*	*Engages the audience in a well-crafted poetic statement that features some powerful imagery and language play*
Meaning • insight • detail • connection to the audience	• undeveloped • more specific detail would improve piece • does not engage audience	• relatively predictable or narrow • some relevant detail • engages the audience, but inconsistently	• thoughtful; deals with topic maturely • carefully chosen details • makes a connection or has an impact on listener – sense of audience	• interesting insights or perspectives • efficient, powerful use of detail • engages the audience through-out – achieves intended effect
Style • poetic devices • vocabulary • voice	• few examples of poetic devices and imagery • basic vocabulary • no real sense of voice	• poetic devices and imagery are often limited to simile, personification, rhyme • appropriate word choice • inconsistent sense of voice	• some effective poetic devices (including sound devices) and imagery • some vitality and variety in language • sense of voice	• original and inventive poetic devices and imagery, with special attention paid to sound devices • effective and powerful word choices; may take risks, be playful • engaging voice
Form • sequence • ending	• illogical sequence • stops abruptly or has an illogical ending	• clear sequence; lacks direction • logical ending; may be obvious or may not offer closure	• clear sequence and direction • satisfying ending with some sense of closure	• sense of direction, building to a conclusion • ending has impact, leaving the audience with something to think about
Presentation • rehearsal and delivery	• more rehearsal needed; more attention needs to be paid to delivery (music, pause, emphasis, expression)	• evidence of some rehearsal; delivery—music (if used), pauses, emphasis, expression—works, but could be played with some more	• rehearsed presentation, careful delivery; music (if used), pauses, emphasis, expression all support the spoken word	• rehearsed presentation, thoughtful delivery; music (if used), pauses, emphasis, expression are all pitch-perfect

Adapted from British Columbia's Writing Performance Standards

CHAPTER 5

Rethinking Reading

When we first got together as a collegial group, we formed a book club focusing on young adult novels. We wanted to know what each other was reading, we wanted to develop wider lists for our literature circles, and we wanted to know what each other thought about those books. We didn't always like the same books, we didn't make the same meaning, and we certainly didn't know what each other was thinking. By listening to one another's responses we got to know each other better and deepened our own understanding of texts we might have dismissed, were it not for the response of a fellow reader. We've all had similar experiences when viewing texts such as films or art works, or listening to a friend's favorite song. The ability to think about texts and discuss them from a diversity of perspectives is absorbing and illuminating.

We want our students to have rich, authentic, real-life reading/viewing/listening experiences like this—enjoyable ones that push them to think, to talk, and to challenge both others and themselves. We want the things we do in our classrooms to mimic what real readers/viewers/listeners do as closely as possible, and so we have made changes over the years in how we teach and ask students to interact with texts and with other readers.

Reading as a Foundation

Reading, along with writing and thinking, is central to English language arts. One could argue, moreover, that reading—and by "reading" we mean print, visual, and aural texts—is the foundation of all we do in the ELA classroom: students must be able to read in order to write, and thinking, while often expressed in writing and speaking, is fed by reading.

Reading, more often than not, is the skill that we as ELA educators fret about the most. We know that if our students cannot read beyond a basic level of comprehension they will suffer many losses in life: loss of educational and career opportunities, loss of dignity, and loss of pleasure. We are, therefore, particularly conscious of the need to provide our students with the skills and experiences they require to be thoughtful and contributing members of our society.

Focusing on Higher-Level Thinking

See page 107 for definition of *text*.

We want to help students move forward in their reading. For some students, moving forward might mean an increase in their overall fluency and enjoyment of reading; for some it might mean thinking critically about the big ideas of a text; for others it might involve making connections among a variety of texts to synthesize new ideas. Ultimately, "students need to go beyond constructing meaning, which is pivotal in the earlier grades, to generating alternative interpretations based on contextual factors" (BC Ministry of Education, 2007: 19). In the end, we want all of our students to be able to create meaning from texts, respond to them, and think critically about them.

We don't wait until the end of a lesson or unit to engage in higher-level thinking activities; rather, by embedding these activities into the reading process, the relevance, value, and importance of a text or task is more readily apparent. Higher-level thinking can be used as an intellectual hook, and when we begin with the big ideas and critical questions, students have a reason for both reading the text and learning about its context.

Core Understandings: Reading

We have explored reading in English language arts in a variety of ways over our careers. Between us, we have had experience teaching reading in the middle years in humanities or science classes, as well as in the secondary grades. We have used highly structured activities or processes to teach students to read strategically. We have used before–during–after formats; we have worked with reading logs and journals; we have done independent reading and literature circles. Regardless of our individual experiences, we have come to some core understandings about reading and about teaching reading.

- We need to know what our students are reading, for what purposes, and how well they are reading various texts.
- Students need to understand why we are asking them to read a given text, and understand any tasks we give them for that reading.
- We need to use what we know about our students' reading to guide reading instruction for the whole class, for small groups, and for individuals.
- We need to model and teach what good readers do.
- Students need to understand that what good readers do varies with the text and the task.
- We need to support our students in reading specific texts for specific tasks.
- Students need opportunities to build meaning with others through discussion.
- We need to support students in thinking critically by asking questions, taking other perspectives, and considering bias.
- Students need to be metacognitive in their reading practice by noting their strengths and challenges, selecting strategies, and setting goals for their reading—with our support.
- Students need choices, whenever possible, of reading material that they can comprehend.
- Students need access to a wide variety of independent reading choices.
- Students need lots of time to read, at school and at home.
- Students need to experience the pleasure of reading often.

These understandings make themselves visible in many ways in our classrooms: whole-class novel studies (usually with shorter books), thematic units, genre-based units, reading workshops, independent reading time, literature circles, reading journals and conferences, cross-curricular units or projects, and more. We have found that these core understanding can provide the basis for any organizational style of teaching.

Helping Students Approach and Negotiate Texts

It's important to note at this point that when we talk about reading, we are talking about reading anything and everything: blogs and websites, videos and artworks, essays and articles, poems and song lyrics, novels and short stories, history and science texts, magazines and newspapers. It's also important to recognize that reading is a complex process and there are many things one can focus on. Louise Rosenblatt (1995), for example, identifies two modes of reading: *efferent* and *aesthetic*. Efferent reading is reading to gather information, to learn something; aesthetic reading is reading primarily for pleasure, to live vicariously through a text.

Readers can approach a text from either stance, and often from both. Sometimes we begin with the aesthetic to get to the efferent, and sometimes we do it the other way around. Working with students to teach them the skills and strategies they need sometimes means taking an efferent stance using a shared text with the whole class. It can also mean taking an aesthetic stance and modeling how an emotional response can sometimes be the way into a text. Regardless of which stance we work from, these responses need to be modeled and shared: it's the teacher's job to model and gradually release the development of complex thinking processes. For this purpose, we will often choose a shorter text, something we can read and work with in one sitting.

Nancie Atwell (2007) calls the state of living through a text being in the "reading zone." If we want our students to get into the zone of reading for pleasure, we need to ensure that, at least some of the time, support from a teacher does not interrupt students' actual reading: once they're in the zone, they really shouldn't want to come out again! Somewhere in our program, we consciously create a space for this type of reading to happen.

Given the range of students in our classrooms—from abilities to interests to attention spans—it is impossible to choose the one book, the one article, the one film, the one inquiry topic that all students will enjoy and engage with.

As much as possible, in all that we do in our classrooms, we try to give students a choice of reading materials—whether that is for a text set of poems, a literature circle, an inquiry circle, or reading workshop. Particularly in reading workshop, we avoid lists of books for students to choose from and instead let them choose books that are accessible to them and that they enjoy. While we use single shared texts to develop knowledge and introduce a strategy, we do not stop there. Inquiry circles, literature circles, and reading workshop provide a place for students to practice the skills they have learned with a shared text. Ultimately, we encourage our students to read widely, and we do our best to put the right text into the hands of the right student. After all, it is by choosing our own texts and reading freely and widely that most of us have become the voracious, thoughtful, and open-minded readers we are today.

While we all recognize the importance of developing students' reading repertoire/strategies, there are many ways to support students in doing this. As we continue to develop our practice and work toward our ultimate goal of developing students' critical literacy, we are negotiating the relationship between teaching reading strategies and fostering reading for pleasure.

Examples from our Classrooms

Leyton and Nicole Widdess use inquiry circles to help students negotiate non-fiction texts. Mehjabeen uses literature circles with a set of novels with a Middle Ages theme for a humanities class. Joanne and Krista use a reading workshop model to give students the opportunity to become immersed in a book.

Across the three examples of sequences that follow, you can see teachers working together to help their students be more successful and passionate learners. We take the idea of being a good reader beyond a mechanical exercise and into the depths of thinking and responding that make reading a rich, personalized, and meaningful experience. There are times when modeling is key and helpful because that is what students need most, but without a focus on student choice and self-regulation, they will not be able to own their meaning-making and strategy use.

Inquiry Circles

An inquiry circle applies a literature circle structure to information text. Members choose to read the same article, chapter, or book in search of information related to questions they have. These are small peer-led discussion groups.

Some key elements of inquiry circles:

Nicole and Leyton have found great success with this format, as students can read and discuss two or three articles a week and use each successive group meeting to clarify and extend their learning.

- Students choose the reading materials from texts that the teacher has introduced (related to themes).
- Students form small groups (active voice vs passive).
- Students keep notes to guide both their reading and discussion (a journal entry, a graphic organizer, sticky notes, annotations in the text).
- Groups meet on a predictable schedule to discuss their reading.
- Topics of inquiry come from the students, not the teachers or textbooks.
- Questions for discussion often emerge while students are working together with the texts.
- Personal responses, connections, and questions are the starting point of discussion.
- The teacher does not lead any group, but acts as a facilitator and observer.
- Groups can share highlights of their reading and thinking with classmates through visuals, presentations, dramatizations, or other means.

In this unit Nicole was teaching a Grade 7/8 combined class. At the time, news media were brimming with stories related to Hurricane Katrina. While the topic of study was supposed to be related to relationships and bullying, conversations in class often turned to hurricane coverage. Thus, a new series of unanticipated questions emerged for shared inquiry. The more Nicole went with the students' fascination with this current event, the more she found they were engaged with the content and the strategies she was introducing. Together Nicole and Leyton corralled this energy into students' reading, discussing, responding to, and summarizing information related to a series of open-ended questions. These ranged from the science-oriented (How do scientists study storms?) to human interest (How do natural disasters impact our lives?) and finally, social responsibility (When disaster strikes, what are our responsibilities?). Their best sources of nonfiction texts included hurricane- related articles from the newspaper and articles from reliable news websites.

The students successfully found links to extreme weather experiences in their personal lives and, in particular, content in their social studies and science classes. However, when Nicole worked with texts on other topics (i.e., fiction and texts in other subject areas), students did not transfer the skills they were building, despite the introduction and modeling of reading strategies through think-alouds, two-column notes, and coding text. Nicole found that students were engaging in instructional activities without being able to explain how they were developing and generalizing strategies.

Thinking Strategies: Starting with Connections

As a Grade 7/8 teacher, Nicole taught all core subjects, which proved useful in the shifting of unit topics. Maintaining their inquiry approach, Leyton and Nicole planned lesson sequences that used open-ended questions and instructional strategies. Open-ended strategies require students to use key thinking skills to find information related to the question of the day or week. Using the Making Connections graphic organizer (page 71), Nicole and Leyton became more explicit with students about the connecting, processing, and transforming/personalizing phases of learning. Nicole used this organizer once or twice a week for about three weeks to get students in the habit of using the targeted thinking skills across texts and classes.

The section on the Making Connections graphic organizer for *3 words* helps students to notice and record three words that were challenging for them during reading, so that Nicole has an idea where word work may need to occur.

See page 71 for the Making Connections graphic organizer.

- She asks the students to think of one main idea they remember from the previous class, one connection they made the previous day, and one question they have for that day's text. In partners, and then as a class, they discuss what students remember, why they think these ideas were important, and finally how their questions relate to these ideas.
- During reading, students are looking and/or listening to make a connection on sticky notes. Nicole asks her students to code the sticky with T–S (text to self), T–T (text to text), and T–W (text to world) (Harvey & Goudvis, 2000).
- The students engage first in partner and then group talk about what they wrote on their sticky notes.
- After discussion, students write two-column notes. In the left column they identify two significant connections they made; on the right side, how their connections relate to what they read.
- Finally, students complete reflection prompts; this allows Nicole and Leyton to get a glimpse of their metacognitive skills.

As Leyton was available to work in Nicole's classroom only once per week, they often used this time to introduce a strategy that Nicole and her students used in different ways over the course of the week.

Text Features

As they moved to their second instructional goal for students, Nicole and Leyton maintained their use of strategies for making connections while introducing skills for using text features.

- Students work in small groups and look through a variety of nonfiction books to generate a list of possible text features and their functions. Students rotate through three different stations of varying nonfiction books and record their findings to share with the rest of the class.
- As Leyton records the ideas on chart paper, Nicole prompts students to be more explicit about the differences between text features. Together the class develops a list of text features and speaks about the functions of each.
- Leyton and Nicole use a two-column format with the headings *Text Feature* and *Function*. Using the two-column notes, students create their own text features reference book. Students are asked to include the text feature and its

function, as well as a visual representation of the text feature to use as a future guide. This becomes a reference when students are note-making using nonfiction material.

Moving on to Inquiry Circles

Nicole felt that the students where successfully using and applying strategies when guided to do so. Students reported understanding what the purpose of a strategy was, but they could not independently apply the strategies effectively when there was no teacher model. Realizing it was time to move on from making connections and text features, but wanting to build on their successes to date, Nicole and Leyton developed an outline for a mini-unit that focused on both determining importance and using inquiry circles. Inquiry circles on topics based on student interests seemed like an excellent way to reinforce the processes introduced in classes related to bullying and Hurricane Katrina, while communicating and reinforcing strategies students could use successfully to learn about topics of interest.

Preparing for Discussion: Showing my Thinking Graphic Organizer

Wanting to see students develop and personalize the thinking strategies they were targeting, Nicole and Leyton developed a graphic organizer to support students as they worked with texts to build their knowledge and define key questions; see the Showing My Thinking graphic organizer on page 72. Students were guided to use the graphic organizer with shared texts and finally with choice texts. Positioning strategy work as part of the preparation for inquiry circle discussions was quite successful in terms of student acquisition and application of these strategies.

This target strategy and graphic organizer required some modeling and guided practice; however, once inquiry groups were established, the focus in the classroom moved away from the teachers.

1. Before reading, students choose a text feature from the reading material to use as they make predictions about the content.
2. During reading, in their inquiry groups, students chunk the text into three sections and decide how they will read the text: independently or taking turns with a partner.
3. Together students complete a magnet note (Buehl, 2001) on a sticky note.
   - Students read the chunk looking for a magnet word, the most important word in that section of the text, and record it in the centre of their sticky note.
   - Then students reread the chunk, looking for the four to five next most important words that attract to the magnet word.
   - After discussion, students record these words on the sticky note around the magnet word. Students do this for multiple chunks of text.
   - The discussion helps students to read and reread nonfiction texts with a focus on determining important information.
4. When they are finished the magnet notes, students individually look for one quote to share in the following day's discussion.
   - Students share a quotation, and each member of the group shares his/her own thinking about that quotation.
   - Then, the first student shares his/her thinking about the quotation—either original ideas or his/her modified thinking based on the group's comments.

The Showing My Thinking graphic organizer (page 72) supported students in using their previous work around text features and also in building the skill of determining importance.

- This process is repeated for each member of the group.
5. The group reviews all their magnet notes and discuss what paragraph heading would capture the main idea of the chunk they have read.
   - Students record the heading on their Showing My Thinking graphic organizer (page 72).
   - After discussion, students (sometimes with support from the adult facilitator) take the paragraph headings and write a summary together.
6. Students independently complete the metacognitive step that requires them to reflect back on their thinking and processes of this activity.

Nicole and Leyton outlined the inquiry circle process and offered topic-related texts based on students' interests. Texts fell into three overarching areas: fashion/beauty myths, sports, and video games. Teacher schedules were arranged so that there was the possibility of having three adults in the room every third lesson to monitor the students' use of strategies. Students were immersed in a process of using and refining target strategies through weekly cycles. Each week there was time for reading and responding to individually chosen novels as well as inquiry group work and discussion.

Leyton and Nicole also identified what mini-lessons were needed by listening to students' conversations. Small group conversations were debriefed as a class then groups set goals for upcoming discussions.

Week	Monday	Tuesday	Thursday

1	• Independent novels
	• Introduce/model readers' response
		• Introduce inquiry circles, Show My Thinking organizer (teacher led)
		• Do with whole class
		  – Model
		  – Practice in info. groups
			• Read independent novel for 20 min.
			• Say Something 5 min.
			• Write response log

2	• Read new article • Fill out Show My Thinking using the magnet strategy – Bring to Tuesday's discussion group	• Say Something (quote & respond to it) • Read chunk, share heading • Repeat until reading is completed • Group summary • Reflection on learning and set goals for reading and next meeting	• Read independent novel for 20 min. • Say Something 5 min. • Write response log
3	• Read new article • Alone or with a partner fill out Show My Thinking using the magnet strategy – Bring to Tuesday's discussion group	• Share headings • Share ideagram criteria • Inquiry groups brainstorm what this might look like • Teacher asks, "What important questions are answered in your article?" (complete inner circle of ideagram) • Groups discuss and create possible ideagram questions	• Read independent novel for 20 min. • Say Something 5 min. • Find section for fluency log 5 min. • Write response log • Complete fluency log and chart it
4	• Review ideagram criteria • Work on centre and outside rings – discuss as a group that items in the outer ring should show specific connections to subheadings	• Work in draft • Students are invited to add an images or icons to their ideagram • Teachers conference with students on ideagram offering descriptive feedback	• Performance-Based Assessment (PBA)

Ideagram: A Summative Assessment

The culminating assignment in this mini-unit was an ideagram (adapted from Brownlie & Feniak, 1998). The purpose of this activity was to help students synthesize their learning about their inquiry topic and to assess student understanding of the material they read. The ideagram is a way for students to show their understanding about a theme, and demonstrate the thinking skills that were explicitly developed during the unit: questioning, working with text features, determining importance, and making connections. When introducing the activity, it is important that students know that the goal of the ideagram is to find relevant information from texts they have read; to make personal, textual, and world connections with the topic; and to demonstrate what they have learned about text features.

See page 73 for the Ideagram template; page 74 for Ideagram Criteria.

INSTRUCTIONS FOR STUDENTS

1. In your inquiry circle, think of some important issues and questions related to sports, beauty myths, or video games. Choose an issue or question that you have learned some information about. Try to choose something that creates a lot of discussion, because there are no easy answers.
2. In the middle of your paper, record the issue or question.
3. In the inside ring, write subheadings that help organize the information.
4. In the middle ring, write quotations from articles that related to the issue or question.
5. In the outside ring (the perimeter of your paper), include additional questions and text-to-self and text-to-world connections you have.

Summative assessments for this unit included students' ideagrams, their reading response logs, and a performance-based assessment of their information reading (see Chapter 3).

Results and Reflections

Looking at the fall and spring nonfiction reading assessments, Nicole and Leyton were pleased to see the gains students made. They were excited that students did well on both the ideagram and the end-of-year reading for information performance assessment. Shifting from the original topic of bullying to the extreme weather theme and then to a choice of inquiry topics engaged students and provided a venue for strategy instruction that students found useful as it helped them prepare for their group discussions and ideagrams.

Literature Circles

Students in the class had been reading independently and working extensively on the reading skills of visualization and making connections. They had also been writing responses in reading journals about what they were reading. By the time this literature circle sequence was taught, students had become skilled users of sticky notes to capture their thinking, and some of the students had begun to create symbolic images to represent their thinking about the texts they were reading.

This literature circle sequence was part of a larger unit taught in Mehjabeen's Humanities 8 class on the European Middle Ages, which was co-planned with Krista, Julie Anne Mainville, Erin Steele, and Catriona Misfeldt.

Using visualization as a skill in reading novels set in the European Middle Ages helped students develop a better understanding of what people's experiences were like during those times. They used their skills of making connections to deepen understanding of the social studies content they learned about by connecting it to the experiences of the characters in their novels. The goals of the literature circle sequence, therefore, were to build on their skills of visualization and making connections, as well as to develop the skills of analysis and writing with evidence. The teachers wanted to have students improve their ability to explain why the images and connections they were making were important. By first learning the key concepts for the unit—"power, interdependence, faith, fealty, fief, and fear"—students were better equipped to connect what was occurring in their novels to the meaningful historical themes they were learning about. These goals tied into the greater goals of the unit, as students worked toward a summative assessment: they researched a topic from the European Middle Ages, making connections between the concepts from the unit and the topic being researched, and representing what they learned in symbolic images.

UNIT THEME

European Middle Ages

ENDURING UNDERSTANDINGS FOR UNIT

1. During the European Middle Ages, daily life, social stratification, and religion were highly structured. These structures created interdependence and sustainability, and power was embedded within them.
2. Feudalism was based on the 4F's: faith, fealty, fiefs, and fear. These were dominant ideas in people's minds and made up their world view.
3. People of the Middle Ages had an inward-looking world view.

UNIT OBJECTIVES

- Students will develop an understanding of the society and perspectives of the people of the European Middle Ages.
- Students will build on the reading skills of visualization and making connections, and develop the skills of analysis and writing with evidence.
- Students will use the skill of questioning to gather information from a variety of texts.

Lessons 1–4: Exploration of the Concepts of *faith, fealty, fief,* and *fear*

To explore the four important concepts that dominated the minds of people living during the European Middle Ages, students work in groups on a variety of learning activities:

FAITH

Students had completed a unit on Judaism, Christianity, and Islam, so in this unit activities focused on the way that faith was integrated into the daily life of each person:

1. a picture study of a map from the European Middle Ages that brought to life how faith was integrated into the world view of the people living in that time
2. developing a calendar of the year that marked all the religious occasions, together with all the other daily/seasonal activities such as harvesting and shearing

FEALTY

Students participate in a simulation of the feudal system.

FIEF

Students develop a visual of a fief using an information text.

Text Set
Crispin: The Cross of Lead, Avi
Sword in the Stone, T.H. White
Girl in a Cage, Jane Yolen and Robert Harris
Angeline, Karleen Bradford
The Midwife's Apprentice, Karen Cushman

The learning sequence shown here focuses only on the literature circle component of this unit and what was taught to set it up. The other concepts (power, interdependence) were frontloaded with activities that used additional information texts.

FEAR

The class watches and analyzes a movie set in the Middle Ages; they discuss what is was that people during that time feared and how it guided their actions.

Lesson 5: Selecting Novels

Two of the texts are not as difficult in their reading level: *The Midwife's Apprentice* and *Crispin*.

• Teacher selection of novels: Five novels are used in this text set. Most of these novels are challenging both in the ideas that they are based on and the level of writing. By this stage in the year, most students are ready for more challenging texts. The literature circle approach also provides them with support in their meaning-making. Mehjabeen keeps copies of other novels set during the European Middle Ages for those students who complete their novels early and want other texts to read. Although students may have read more than one text during the unit, they analyze a single text in their groups in order to develop a deeper understanding.
• Student selection of novels: The first step in the literature circle sequence is to have students select the novel they will read. To facilitate this, Mehjabeen reads out a section (the first two paragraphs) and provides a synopsis for each novel. She also highlights the structure and techniques of each of the authors, as some of the novels have non-linear or more challenging narrative structures. Students are then able to select the novel that both interests them and is at the appropriate level of challenge.
• Starting the process, independent reading: Students are asked to read the first chapter and to mark their sticky notes with images, connections, or significant quotations. These are all skills that they have developed in previous months.

Lessons 6–7: Meeting with the Literature Circle Group

The following day, students come together in their literature circle groups. Their task for the day is to share what they recorded in a discussion and to complete a graphic organizer together.

See page 75 for the Literature Circles Discussion Organizer.

• Mehjabeen models the completion of a graphic organizer, using a film that the class had watched together, *Joan of Arc*. She invites the class to fill it out with her. In the modeling, she highlights the process of explaining why the image, connection, or quotation is important.
• Groups engage in discussion about the first chapter of their novels and complete the graphic organizer together.

Lessons 8–10: Feedback and Repeat; Assessment

• The next day, Mehjabeen returns the graphic organizers to each group with her feedback. The group has to revise or add to the organizer based on that feedback.
• Mehjabeen models how the format of the graphic organizer will become the format for their reading journals. For each journal entry, students are asked to select three of their sticky notes, to stick them into their journal, and to explain why the image, quotation, or connection is important.

- Mehjabeen models the writing of these responses on the overhead for three classes, each day using an image, connection, or quotation.
- Students continue to come together to discuss their novels and to work on their responses.
- Assessment: Students hand in their reading journals. Students write two or three responses and receive feedback before being given a mark.

Lessons 11 and Beyond: Connecting Reading and Concepts from Social Studies

- Students continue the process of reading, marking sticky notes, and writing responses, until they finish their novels.
- Every few days, Mehjabeen introduces another graphic organizer that relates to one of the concepts being explored in the unit.

SAMPLE LITERATURE CIRCLES DISCUSSION GUIDE: FEAR

In each of your novels, your characters are experiencing some kind of fear. As we have been studying the Middle Ages in Europe, we have seen that there are many things that the people in that time feared. In your group, discuss the different things that your characters fear and fill out the table below :

In our book, the main character or all the characters fear :	Quote or example that shows that he/she/they fear this (include page number):	Why is this thing feared?	How does this connect to any of the other ideas we are thinking about such as: Power, Interdependence, Fief, Faith or Fealty ?

- At the end of the unit, students complete an independent research project on a topic of interest on the European Middle Ages. A component of the summative task requires them to create images and write paragraphs that show how their topic connects to the concepts that they have been learning about (power, interdependence, faith, fealty, fief, and fear).

Setting Goals in Reading Workshop

In their English classes, Krista and Joanne have a reading workshop unit that runs all year, weaving through their other units, about once every fifth class. In reading workshop, students choose their own books (fiction and narrative non-fiction) and set reading goals for each term of the school year. Reading workshop class includes time for reading, as well as a mini-lesson on a reading skill or a shared poem, and time to work on formative and summative assessments for the workshop, such as letter-essays (adapted from Atwell, 2007).

One of the most powerful things that Joanne and Krista do in their reading workshop—second only to giving students the freedom to read what they like and abandon what they don't—is to have each student set his or her own reading goal, monitor his or her progress, and reflect at the end of each term in a reading goal self-evaluation, which is summatively assessed.

After introducing the reading workshop at the beginning of the school year and establishing routines, Krista and Joanne generally follow the same sequence in each term:

We have students set goals in order to facilitate metacognition as well as to nurture a love of reading and a knowledge of themselves as readers.

1. Students brainstorm and review possible reading goals.
   • "Reading faster" is the only unacceptable goal, as it typically leads to skipping, skimming, and misreading.
2. As students progress through the year, Krista and Joanne suggest more challenging goals, moving from setting numbers of books or pages to goals involving deeper comprehension, analysis, connections, and more challenging books.
   • Students are taught how to determine if a book is right for them, and to "level" each book they read as a *holiday*, *just right*, or *challenging* book (from Atwell, 2007).
3. Students set a reading goal for the term and hand it in for teacher feedback, using the Reading Workshop: Reading Goal sheet, page 76.
   • Students are asked to make goals specific, measurable, achievable, reasonable, and time-limited (one school term).
4. Once goals are approved, students develop a plan to help themselves meet the goal.
   • Students may need a mini-lesson in making a specific, practical plan.
5. Three times each term, students do a check-in to reflect on successes, struggles, and what changes they might need to make, and to receive feedback from the teacher.
   • Feedback includes suggestions to change goals to make them easier or more challenging, "permission" to abandon books they don't like, or tips to help students find time to read or deal with challenging vocabulary.
6. At the end of the term, students use the Reading Goal sheet to write a reading goal self-evaluation, which is used to generate a mark.
   • Students who do not reach a goal—for whatever reason—are not penalized. They get a mark for their *reflection* on their struggles, successes, and progress as readers.

See page 76 for the Reading Workshop: Reading Goal Sheet

One benefit of having students set reading goals for each term, rather than for the whole year or semester, is that they get to practice setting goals, working toward them, and reflecting on them. By the third term, students are quite eloquent in their reflections on their growth as readers, as you can see from these comments by Grade 8 students:

"…[E]ven though it was a struggle for me to understand the books, I still managed to understand them. It took a lot of effort and time for me to search up the words, to reflect on the chapter and to try to decipher the meaning, but eventually, I still succeeded in understanding the books. I found that…a huge accomplishment."

"This term's goal [trying to achieve a higher understanding of books rather than just reading and finishing them] wasn't only for this term, but was actually for life… I want to satisfy my thirst for excellent books."

"Looking back now, I think that my term 2 reading goal [to read 28 books] was a very bad reading goal because as long as I read and understand the texts, then it shouldn't matter how many books I read."

"This goal [reflecting, connecting and focusing] helped me grow and it guided me into a more *self-actualized* character. This is probably the biggest success of this goal because I didn't only do something for the assignment, I also did something for *myself*."

Making Connections

Connecting

Main Idea:	Connection:	Connection:

Processing

Sticky Note 1	Sticky Note 2	Sticky Note 3

Personalizing/Transforming

Connection	My Thinking

Metacognition

I want you to notice how I…
For next time, I want to…
3 words I want to add: •   •   •

Showing My Thinking

Connecting	Text feature: _____

Processing	Chunk 1 Paragraph Heading: Sticky note(s)
	Chunk 2 Paragraph Heading: Sticky note(s)
	Chunk 3 Paragraph Heading: Sticky note(s)

Personalizing/ Transforming	Summary
	What I want you to notice about my thinking Next time, I plan to… (goal setting)

Ideagram

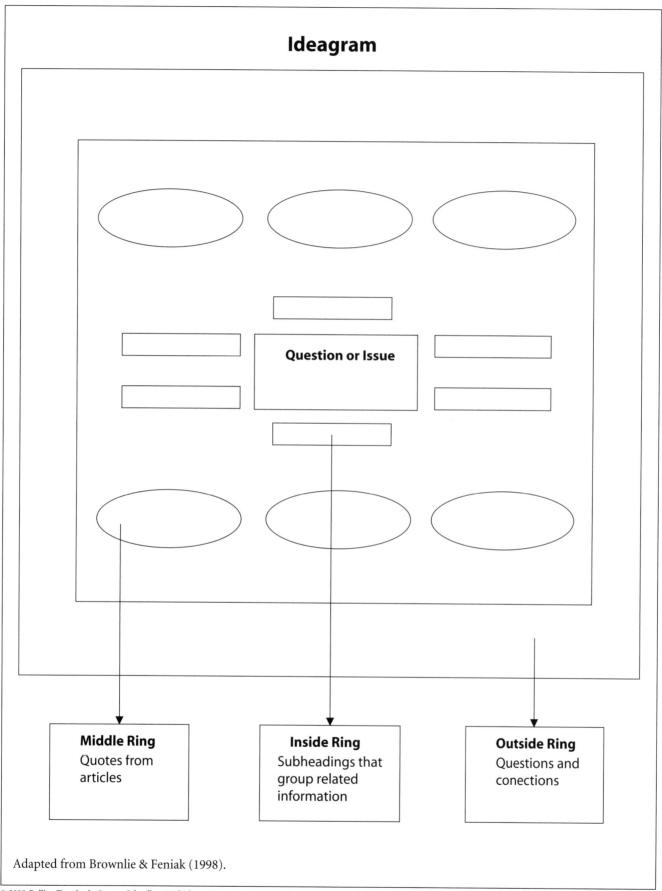

Question or Issue

Middle Ring
Quotes from articles

Inside Ring
Subheadings that group related information

Outside Ring
Questions and conections

Adapted from Brownlie & Feniak (1998).

Information Circle Ideagram Criteria

Mark	Criteria
4	• Question is open-ended and related to topic • Several logical subheadings are used to organize information related to question • At least two relevant quotations are used to support each subheading • Includes several connections to other articles, news, stories • Several personal connections are included (personal experiences, prior knowledge, opinions)
3	• Question is open-ended and related to topic • Most subheadings are used to effectively to organize information related to question • Some mostly relevant quotations are used to support subheadings • Makes some connections to other articles • Some personal connections are included (personal experiences, prior knowledge)
2	• Question is too narrow and/or not clearly related to info circle topic • Not clear how some subheadings are related to question • Quotations are not specifically related to subheadings • Few connections to other articles • Few personal connections
1	• Limited response, subheadings are missing or not used to group information • Few to no quotations and/or connections from other articles • Few to no personal connections

Literature Circles Discussion Organizer

Text (film, novel) Title: _____

Group Members: _____

In your group, discuss the assigned section of the text and then complete the table below:

Do the task listed	Explain why you think it is important
Draw one picture that summarizes one of the important things that happened in the section	
Write one quotation from your text	
Write one connection that your group made	
Write 3 questions that your group has about the book so far	
Which of the following words best describes the feelings of your character: loneliness, despair, fear, pathetic? (Look up the words if you do not understand them.)	Explain your choice of word.

Reading Workshop: Reading Goal

English _____ Reading Goal for Term_____

My reading goal is…

I chose this goal because…

Plan for My Reading Goal

Thinking About My Progress

Metacognition Questions	Check-In #1 Date:	Check-In #2 Date:	Check-In #3 Date:
• Where am I in my reading goal? • What successes have I had so far?			
• What am I struggling with? • Why is this difficult for me?			
• What do I need to change or do so that I can be successful?			
Teacher feedback (comments & suggestions)			

CHAPTER 6

Writing as Thinking

All four of us remember our initial academic writing experiences and our first forays into teaching writing. Krista reflects:

> When I think back to my university career, I remember few pieces of the writing I did. I certainly don't remember anything about the essays I began at nine pm the night before they were due, and handed in, still hot from the printer, the following morning. What I do remember are the pieces I paid attention to, took time crafting, and revised. These are the pieces that I still use as samples for my students, or that I'll reread from time to time for my own enjoyment.
>
> Why I didn't learn from my own experience as a student, I'll never know, but it wasn't until a few years into my career that I changed my exhausting and mostly fruitless practice in writing instruction. In hindsight, I realize why I never had any classroom management problems in my first year or two of teaching, as many young teachers do. I assigned so much work that my students barely had a chance to breathe—they were writing all of the time, first draft after first draft. I didn't instruct so much as I assigned, collected, carried marking home, carried it back, assigned, collected, carried increasingly heavy bins to and from home, assigned, collected, then pulled all-nighters the week before my marks were due.
>
> I remember an essay unit I did with my Grade 11 students—a quick one at the beginning of the year, where they wrote an expository essay, a narrative essay, a descriptive essay, and a literary analysis essay. I've just outlined a year's worth of work, and we "completed" it in two months. I also remember the unit I gave those poor English 12 students who had me instead of their sane teacher for 13 weeks during my practicum. For our study of *All Quiet on the Western Front*, I created a sheet of 12 writing assignments, from which students were to choose four. These weren't minor. They ranged from a research report on weapon use in WW1, to an argumentative essay on chance, to a comparison essay using Timothy Findlay's *The Wars*. We studied the novel, but I gave little to no instruction on the multitude of writing forms I was asking students to use. I was, at the time, happy with the assignment because I felt it gave them choice, but I can guarantee that none of these students has kept any of this work to reread, and I taught them precious little about how to write.

We each have our own stories of how we have come to refine and change the ways we teach writing to be more explicit and learning-oriented. Thankfully, we've moved forward, albeit from different places based on our own strengths and experiences. How best to teach students to write is a question we continue to think about and discuss. It is central to the life of an English teacher: no other work spills over into our weekends and evenings as much as writing assessment does. The dreaded piles of marking; the tension that lies in wanting to give students valuable feedback in order to help them improve, while at the same time maintaining a semblance of balance in our lives.

Core Understandings: Writing

- We need to use what we know about our students' writing to guide writing instruction for the whole class, for small groups, and for individuals.
- We need to help student writers develop as critical thinkers who ask themselves about the purpose and impact of their writing.
- We need to model and teach what good writers do.
- Students need to understand that what good writers do varies with the form and the task.
- Students need constructive responses to their writing.
- Students need opportunities to build meaning and share approaches with others through discussion.
- Students need to be metacognitive in their writing practice by noting their strengths and challenges, selecting strategies, and setting goals for their writing—with our support.
- Students need multiple and varied invitations to write in class.
- When possible, students need choices regarding form and content in order to help them develop writing identities.
- Students need to understand the value of revision.
- Students need to understand the multiple phases in the writing process and that the process is recursive.
- Students need to have opportunities to play with language in order to support the development of style and voice.
- We need to teach grammar in context, as it relates specifically to student needs.
- We need to encourage students to read a lot, and with a writer's eye.
- Evaluation of writing should give the writer the tools and techniques to develop both their strengths and areas of challenge.

Writing For and With Students

Most of us are more comfortable modeling how we read challenging texts than modeling writing. It's somehow more daunting to create a text in front of others. But it's such a rich experience for students to be able to see the time it takes for us to come up with a workable thesis statement, or a title for a poem, or a conclusion for a memoir.

In order to teach with these ideas in mind, we've had to learn to slow down. That doesn't mean that we don't ask our students to write a lot—we do. What it does mean is that not all writing goes through all stages of the writing process, and not all is summatively assessed for meaning, form, style, *and* conventions. It also means that we practice making the often-invisible struggle of wrangling thoughts into words visible. We model throughout the writing process, from brainstorming through publishing, trying to make the work we do in front of students as authentic as possible. To do so, we need to put ourselves in the position of our students.

Writing experts agree that, to develop a society where educated people communicate effectively, teachers and administrators need to "value, understand and practice writing themselves" (NWP and Nagin, 2003: 60). We can't expect students to take risks if we're not willing to. Depending on what we're teaching, we might ask students to assign us a topic, or give us a range of choices. We model our own process, going through each step in front of them, from brainstorming ideas around the topic, to organizing these ideas, to checking back to ensure we've understood the task, to pausing to consider the elements of form or the knowledge and expectations of the audience, all the while thinking aloud as we try to make our own approaches to writing transparent. This also makes explicit how recursive the writing process is.

We don't model the writing process from beginning to end every time we engage in writing instruction, but it's powerful to do once in a while to show students how challenging writing can be and how we can work through the challenges. If we're teaching a particular form that we're going to be engaging with over time, we might take students through an entire process step by step. We would model the gathering and organization of ideas, and then students would gather and organize their ideas with support. Next, we would begin our draft, after which we would support students as they wrote theirs…and so on, through the revision and editing process. If we don't feel comfortable drafting from scratch in front of our students, or don't have the time, we can still model revision authentically. We can take them through revision strategies step by step, beginning with a piece we've written, and then asking students to work with other samples, their peers' work, and their own work. We can do similar work with editing.

This slower pace may mean that students take four to six weeks (in a linear year) to work through an essay, and another six weeks to write a memoir. It also means that we are teaching writing instead of merely assigning it. Graham and Perrin (cited in BC Ministry of Education, 2007: 37) note that "teaching adolescents strategies for planning, revising, and editing their compositions has shown a dramatic effect on the quality of students' writing." Woven into this time would be mini-lessons targeting specific skills; lots of class time to analyze models, to build and work with criteria, and to draft and conference with peers and with the teacher; guided revision sessions; and opportunities for publication. We want students to craft pieces they can be proud of. We find that taking the time to model, discuss, and revise with a specific focus in mind helps students to apply these ideas. It also makes assessment more meaningful for students. We focus our assessment, both formative and summative, on the aspects of writing we have actually taught.

Another crucial aspect of writing instruction is developing a community of writers. Writing is not something we do in isolation. From shared brainstorming during prewriting and drafting, to examining models together, to developing criteria, to peer editing, to sharing our work, writers work together. Apart from a personal journal (and the advent of the blog is changing even this), very little real-world writing is written entirely alone and shared with no one. For us, students sharing ideas and approaches, and conferencing with one another on their ongoing writing, is just as important as teacher modeling and feedback. One of the benefits of having a community of writers in the classroom is that the teacher is no longer the sole source of feedback. When responding to writing becomes a shared responsibility, this can both lighten the teacher's marking load and empower students to deepen their reflection about what makes writing effective.

As one student put it: "When I saw [my teacher] edit her… piece with the class, she crossed out lots and even started taking a different path. If English teachers do it, it must be okay, right?"

One of the very best ways to engage students in reflective and personalized revision is through one-on-one conferences. While it is a challenge to find the time for individual writing conferences, particularly with a class of 30 students, any effort to work individually with students, even for a few minutes each, is worthwhile.

When we create structures that value student writing, students learn the joy that comes with creating texts and garnering response.

Writing as Critical Thinking

Noted teacher-researcher Linda Rief (2006: 33) points out that "there is no one process that defines the way all writers write." While writing is a recursive process, this happens for different writers in different ways. The more opportunities students have to talk through and reflect on their approaches and draw from the ideas of others, the more likely they are to personalize and extend their writing practice:

> Studies of how writers actually work show them shuffling through phases of planning, reflection, drafting and revision, though rarely in a linear fashion. Each phase requires problem-solving and critical thinking. (NWP and Carl Nagin, 2003: 34)

When students write about, read, and revise their ideas, they are engaged in a recursive process of critical thinking.

Transforming thoughts into text engages students in higher-level thinking. We create opportunities for students to record and reflect on their beliefs, impressions, and experiences to help them learn about themselves, and as a means to develop their ability to communicate effectively. When students collect their thoughts and responses, they have something concrete to analyze and discuss. By looking at their responses critically, students can examine their beliefs, attitudes, biases, and perspectives related to a range of issues or topics. They can also consider if and how the process of creating text has altered or refined their opinions. (We explore this further in Chapter 8.)

When we share our writing with each other (student to student, teacher to student, student to teacher), we can revise our writing to communicate more effectively. Engaging in a process of sharing and analyzing one another's work helps to nurture a workshop-like environment. Students critique and revise their own and others' communications and develop a disposition where they constantly ask themselves, "Where to next?" They can ask one another questions like these:

- How might you push your thinking about this idea or issue?
- Have you supported your opinions? With what types of evidence?
- Have you explained your ideas clearly?
- Have you considered multiple perspectives? Which ones have you left out? Why? How does this affect your communication?
- What is your bias and how does it come through?

We need to make the purposes for writing clear to students, and writing for audiences can help engage students in the writing process. Our writing can and should take many forms. We want to make sure the writing students do is not simply "for school" writing. We want them to see its application to their learning about topics of interest and about themselves.

We believe that students' development as writers and readers is grounded in their development as thinkers. We want them to shape and communicate ideas with real audiences and purposes in mind. In this book we talk about thematic teaching, where students explore ideas and develop enduring understandings. Writing is central to this process of inquiry. Rather than asking students to come up with predetermined understandings, we want them to draw their own conclusions from readings and discussions. Our role is to help them develop the skills needed to contemplate big ideas and issues. To keep the focus of writing assignments authentic and thinking-oriented we encourage students to share and examine their beliefs, feelings, discoveries, opinions, and stories. This is, of course, reflected in the criteria we use to give students feedback. The central focus of any work we do with criteria is to give students feedback that is as descriptive as possible and that will help them to improve their communications. Well-written criteria that are understood by both students and teachers will have the added benefit of helping teachers summatively assess work.

In the examples from our classrooms that follow, we show how we help students to develop a practice of "writing as thinking." To do this they need to read examples of the genre or style they are working with; engage in conversations about what is effective and possible; and select, develop, and apply approaches in the service of what they think, feel, or believe about texts, ideas, and/or issues. We show how our assessment is related to what we focus on in our teaching, which in turn comes from the needs of our students and the demands of the form within which we are working.

> As we get better at integrating our planning, assessment, and instruction, we find that we are getting better at teaching "writing as reading" and "writing as thinking" by which students learn about their and others' authoring cycles and develop a personalized practice.

Examples from our Classrooms

The shift in our practice from giving assignments and instructions to modeling processes and providing explicit instruction, along with assigning fewer writing tasks that are more thoroughly reworked by students, has had an impact on our assessment: we spend more time giving feedback when it matters, and less time agonizing over giving marks. By the time we put a grade on a piece of writing, we have usually seen it at least once, identified strengths and problems in our students' writing, and delivered mini-lessons that have given students the skills they need to be successful in the task. We begin with two sequences on explicitly teaching analytical writing, followed by four processes for revision.

Explicit Teaching of Literary Analysis

> When it came time to teach students how to write a short story analysis essay, we found that we needed to support them a bit less. We modeled how to build an outline but we did not need to show them step-by-step how to write the essay; students were able to transfer what they had learned from writing the poetry analysis paragraphs to their essays.

Joanne and Krista were able to co-teach this particular sequence as part of a larger unit they co-planned on the concept of story, in which they looked at poetry, short stories, spoken word, and personal narratives. Prior to this sequence, students had read a number of short stories as a whole class, and worked in small groups on a set of poems in literature circles (see Chapter 4). With this building of prior knowledge and thinking time, Krista and Joanne felt confident that students could be successful with an in-class demand writing task.

The purpose of these lessons was to explicitly model and teach students how to write a short literary analysis. Krista and Joanne chose to focus on poetry first because students had just finished looking at poetry in small groups; all of the poems were related in some way to the idea of story. Students then wrote an analysis on the short stories they had looked at together prior to the poetry literature circles.

Lesson 1: Poetry Analysis

1. Krista and Joanne prepare the lesson by brainstorming some common poetry analysis prompts: discuss the contrast in the poem, discuss the conflict in the poem, discuss the experience of the speaker, discuss the symbolism in the poem. They write these prompts on the board.
   - They photocopy Leona Gom's poem "Guilt" complete with text markings they did in preparation for a fishbowl discussion (see Chapter 4).

- They give students some time to familiarize themselves with the poem and the initial comments before beginning.

2. Krista and Joanne ask the class to assign one of the four analysis topics written on the board.
   - In pairs, students choose a poem from their literature circle sets (students discussed three poems in small groups and reflected on them, so they are familiar with the poems).
   - Once students have a poem to work with, they also choose an analysis topic from the four written on the board.

3. Krista and Joanne discuss what the topic means in the context of the poem, creating a more specific topic based on the generic one they are assigned.
   - In pairs, students do the same thing, and Krista and Joanne support students in their narrowing of their topic.

4. Krista and Joanne stand at the board, each with a marker in hand, and think aloud about their process as they try to articulate a thesis statement.
   - They brainstorm ideas connected to the topic, and make notes on the board, sometimes backtracking and crossing things out, often asking each other clarifying questions.
   - Once the teachers arrive at a thesis statement, they share their sense of accomplishment with the students.
   - Students work with their partners to create a thesis statement.

5. Krista and Joanne make a two- or three-paragraph outline for their poem analysis.
   - They invite the students to do the same, moving around the classroom to provide support.
   - Once everyone is on their way, Krista and Joanne go back to the front of the room and, beginning with their thesis statement, write the first paragraph of their analysis, thinking aloud throughout the process.
   - Students return to their work and write their drafts.
   - In preparation for the next lesson, Krista collects the students' drafts and creates a sample analysis paragraph to share with students.

Lesson 2: Assessment

1. In preparation for this lesson, Krista and Joanne mark the students' poetry analyses, using a six-point scale, but with no descriptive feedback.
   - They complete one of the poetry analyses they had begun (when modeling in front of the students, they completed only the first paragraphs), evaluate it, and analyze it using a chart they have prepared for the students to use (see Sample Analysis Paragraph and Sample Assessment and Evidence Sheet on page 83).
   - Partway through their analysis, Krista and Joanne realize they don't entirely agree with their interpretation of the poem, so their paper ends up with a 5 on their six-point scale. They find evidence of some of the criteria from each of the 4, 5, and 6 criteria rubrics, and use that to fill in their assessment evidence chart.

2. In class, Krista and Joanne show the students their completed analysis of the poem and their assessment evidence chart.
   - This provides a good opportunity to talk about what they missed and how they might have improved their paper.

Krista had three English 12 classes—Krista and Joanne wanted to be thinking about a new topic in front of each class, and to model the process of writing an analysis from scratch each time they were with a different group of students.

There were moments in the modeling process when the teachers drew a blank and felt vulnerable; it was valuable for the students to see the struggle that's often involved with developing a precise, thoughtful thesis statement.

- Students do the same thing: they look for phrases from the number that corresponds to the grade they are assigned, as well as to the one above and below. Students complete these charts together and submit them for feedback.
- The summative grade comes from the short story analysis essay students would write later, but Krista and Joanne want everyone to go through the process of analyzing a poem and reflecting on their work.

SAMPLE ANALYSIS PARAGRAPH

Straightforward examples of guilt, in the first stanza of Gom's poem, "Guilt," are contrasted with its complex effects in the second stanza. In the beginning, although the speaker is clearly feeling some guilt about what she has done to the people in her life, she is able to walk away from each individual incident. She knows that she has been wrong: she says she can "never forget/ her [mother's] hurt face turning away," and she finds her father's missing "damned magazine" in her room. All the same, she never admits guilt or apologizes. The guilt in each example is brief and fleeting, and easy to get over. The power of these examples is that readers can see themselves in one or more of them; they are all common and often repeated.

The complexity of the guilt is revealed in the way the speaker experiences it well after the events are over. Many people would brush off similar interactions, and never think of them again. Each individual incident in the first stanza is one that could potentially be forgotten, but none is, and they turn themselves into the "little knots" that never seem to leave her; in fact, they add to one another until there are "thousands of them." So begins a stanza laden with imagery that compares the accumulation of guilt—the knots that become lumps—to a malignancy. The language in the second stanza is heavy; there are no anecdotes, there is no narration. It is reflective and yet somehow hopeless in the sense that the guilt is a terminal illness, one that will "[keep] her sick" for as long as she lives. The seemingly simple examples of everyday hurtful events have become a devastating disease.

SAMPLE ASSESSMENT AND EVIDENCE SHEET

Type of writing assignment:___*Analytical poetry paragraph*___

Topic/Title:___*Discuss the use of contrast in the poem, "Guilt"*___

Score:__5__

Assessment criteria met in the writing (quote criteria)	Evidence that the writing has met the selected assessment criteria (quote from writing/explain it)
6—The writing style demonstrates a sophisticated use of language	• "Each individual…'thousands of them'."—use of ; and two short quotations • "So begins…malignancy."—turn of phrase, use of dash • "The language…narrator."— parallelism
5—The response reflects a strong grasp of the topic	• "Straightforward examples…second stanza."—clear thesis • refers to the two contrasted stanzas regularly • conclusion shows the whole paper was on topic
5—The response reflects a strong grasp of the…poem	• "The guilt in each example is brief and fleeting, and easy to get over."—really? This may not be correct, therefore this is not a 6 paper • "So begins…malignancy."—shows grasp of imagery • "The language in the second stanza is heavy…" to end of paragraph—shows complexity of poem
4—References are present and appropriate	• Could have not had any references and this wouldn't have made much of a difference • Only 5 quotations, but they are well-integrated • Quotations tend to be too short (4/5 are only 2–3 words long vs. 5–10 words long)

Assessment criteria met in the writing (quote criteria)	Evidence that the writing has met the selected assessment criteria (quote from writing/explain it)
6—Clear and precise writing	• "Many people would brush off similar interactions, and never think of them again"—pronouns have clear antecedents • "The power of…often repeated"— precise language; a statement is given and explained
Goals: What will you focus on explicitly to improve your work?	• Talk through our understanding of the poem more to make sure we didn't miss anything • Add more purposeful references and discuss them in more detail • Make conclusion more engaging or thoughtful, not just on topic

Lesson 3: Short Story Analysis

Steps in the Writing Process
1. Mark the Text
2. Generate a Thesis
3. Brainstorm Ideas
4. Organize/Order the Brainstorm
5. Write Your Draft
6. Revise Your Draft
7. Edit Your Work

1. To prepare for this lesson, Krista and Joanne write an outline for a short story analysis essay on humor, using Dorothy Parker's "You Were Perfectly Fine."
   • They save their brainstorming sheets to share with the students, in addition to their final outline.
2. They begin the lesson by having the students read "You Were Perfectly Fine."
   • Students brainstorm in small groups how Dorothy Parker creates humor in the story.
   • Krista and Joanne share their brainstorm, and follow this up with their draft outline.
3. With a partner, students write a practice outline for an analytical essay on this prompt: *With reference to "You Were Perfectly Fine," discuss contrast.*
   • Krista and Joanne have students use the same story to create an outline on a different topic as a way to scaffold their learning.

MODEL BRAINSTORM FOR A SHORT STORY ANALYSIS

Prompt: In multi-paragraph essay form and with reference to "You Were Perfectly Fine," discuss humor.

1. Mark the Text
   We went through the short story and identified techniques authors often use to create humor. We found repetition, hyperbole, litotes, sarcasm, irony, self- deprecation, contrast, juxtaposition… After we looked at our notes, we noticed that the author uses a lot of contrast. This led to our thesis.

2. Thesis
   Dorothy Parker uses contrast to create humor in her short story, "You Were Perfectly Fine."

3. Brainstorm Ideas that relate to/support the thesis
   Then we brainstormed the types of contrast she uses.

4. Organize/Order the Brainstorm
   • description of characters
     - he "eased himself into the low chair, and rolled his head to the side"
     - she's "clear-eyed…sitting light and erect…smil[ing] brightly"
   • types of speech used by the two characters
     - he asks questions: "Did I do any other fascinating tricks at dinner?"
     - she provides the answers
   • length of speech

- she always talks more than he does
- figures of speech used by the two characters
  - Parker often gives him lines full of sarcasm and irony: "That must have been a treat. I sang."
  - Parker often gives her lines full of litotes: "She only got a little tiny bit annoyed just once, when you poured the clam-juice down her back." She also uses hyperbole a lot: "I think it would simply kill me" (if you didn't remember the ride in the taxi).
- there's contrast within her speeches
  - "They loved it." (his singing) - and then a couple of lines later – "everybody kept shushing you."
  - The maitre d'hotel "didn't care a bit" (about Peter's singing), but "he was afraid they'd close the place again, if there was so much noise."
- there's a contrast between her understanding/retelling of the events with his dawning grasp of events (she understands all…he's slowly getting there)
- there's a fundamental contrast between her line, "You were perfectly fine" and his interpretation of the events – he's slowly realizing how "unfine" he is
- repetition of phrases
  - he repeats: "Oh, dear, oh, dear, oh, dear."
  - she repeats: "You were perfectly fine/absolutely all right."
5. Write Your Draft
6. Revise Your Draft
7. Edit Your Work

Lesson 4: Student Writing and Feedback

The student could choose between two topics for their analytical essay on the short story:
Discuss conflict in Gina Berriault's "The Stone Boy."
Discuss humor in Dorothy Parker's "Here We Are."

1. Students had two class blocks to write an analytical essay on one of two short stories they had discussed earlier in the unit.
   - Students were able to share their work with each other during the first block, and were able to ask Krista for help during the entire writing process.
2. These essays were much more readable and well-crafted than the previous literary essays students had written.
   - When students received their marked papers, they had the opportunity of coming in at lunch to rewrite them, taking into consideration teacher feedback.

Revision

Krista and Joanne have tried multiple methods to revise work with their students. The strategies detailed below move from the most formal and structured to the most informal and discussion-oriented. We begin with a look at whole-class revision, followed by individual and peer checklists, writers' workshop, and writers' circles.

Whole-Class Revision

When Joanne is working with students on a written piece—an essay, a memoir, or a poem—she often uses whole-class revision. In this process, students have the opportunity to review and revise their work in a process, as well as how to determine if their work is meeting the expectations of the criteria.

- Before doing whole-class revision, Joanne takes students through a process of prewriting, often with a graphic organizer to help draw out students' thinking, and drafting. Students have also created or reviewed the criteria for the writing task by this point in the process.

- To prepare, Joanne reviews the criteria for the assignment and looks at the column for fully meeting expectations. For each aspect (such as meaning, style, form, or conventions) there are usually several bulleted points. Beginning with the meaning aspect, Joanne creates an overhead of instructions to help students find and mark evidence of each bullet in their work. An example of instructions for a memoir is below.

WHOLE-CLASS REVISION PROCESS: MEANING

- Put a box around every **feeling/emotion** word/phrase.
  - Are the feelings specific, or did you just "feel good/bad"? What other words can you use?
  - What other ways can you show your feelings—physical symptoms, comparisons…
- Put a circle around every **thought** you express about what happened (words/phrases)
  - Are your thoughts and feelings given throughout the memoir or all in one place?
  - Why did you make that choice? Is it effective?
- Every time you describe a **sense** (what *you* see, hear, touch, smell, taste, or an action you do), underline it and put an "S" above it.
- Every time you give a **detail** other than a sense (e.g., example, explanation, background information, or description), underline it and put a "D" above it.
  - Where are your senses and details? Are they throughout the memoir or all in one place?
  - Do you describe them specifically? Are they effective?
- At the end of your draft, write down the point, message, or "So what?" you are trying to get across; below that, write the sentences from the draft that you think help to get it across, or write some to put into your next draft.

For example, if students must "express feelings," as part of the Meaning expectations, she explains that *anger* might be expressed using
- Feeling words: *mad, angry* or *furious*
- Descriptions of the physical sensation of anger: *my heart was pounding, my fists clenched, and I couldn't hear anything except my enemy's laughter*
- Similes or metaphors: *I was a pot on the stove, steaming and rattling, ready to boil over*

Editing of conventions is always the last class, and follows one or two classes of peer-revision after the whole-class revision days. By this time it is very clear to students how editing differs from revision and they can see the value and purpose of both. More importantly, they have begun to develop the habit of critically rereading their writing multiple times, with a specific focus for each review—just like "real" writers do.

- In class, students are also prepared: they have brought in the latest draft of their piece, and have highlighters and pens at the ready. First, Joanne reviews the criteria that students will focus on in that class—typically just one aspect of the rubric, such as meaning. Then she puts up the overhead of revision instructions and shows the first bullet. Joanne explains what that criterion might look like in their writing.
- Once students know what to look for, they reread their pieces and code the text using the suggested instructions. As an alternative, students can color-code their work with highlighters or create their own code (and key). If students find that they are missing an example of a particular point, they make a note to work on that part of the criteria.
- Joanne leads students through the overhead, allowing students a few minutes to read their work and code their writing. Not all students will be able to do a thorough review at this point, which is fine; the important thing is that students are very clear about what they are looking for in their work.
- Once the whole class has gone through the overhead, Joanne gives students time to work independently to review their work, using the overhead as a reference. Most students are able to do this work on their own; some students struggle when it comes to finding a "big idea" and may need help from a peer or from Joanne.
- By the end of the first whole-class revision block, on just one aspect of the criteria, Joanne always asks students if they have found anything in their pieces that they can work on—nearly every hand shoots up, every time. Students can easily see the value in this activity and its immediate impact on their writing, and when they are asked to make revisions on their drafts and

bring a "clean" draft next class for the second round of whole-class revision, most students do so willingly, knowing that their pieces will be better for it.

- For the next class, Joanne prepares another overhead with instructions for specific things that students need to have in the piece, drawn from the criteria rubric. Depending on the type of writing and the focus of instruction, Joanne may combine form and style or separate them.

Individual and Peer Revision Checklists

Krista often creates revision checklists for her students, patterned after a rubric. See below for an example of a rubric she used for a free verse poem. Two checklists follow: the first for the *Style* category in the rubric, the second for the *Form* category. She asks questions that address each of the bulleted criteria, making it clear what students can do to improve in a given area. These checklists can be adapted for peer revision, with a few word changes; see page 88 for an example of a peer revision checklist for style, based on this same rubric.

- When students have completed a working draft of a piece, Krista will often begin the revision process with the peer revision form. Groups of three work well. Krista makes two copies of a peer revision form to be stapled to each draft so that, once the rotation is complete, each student author will have feedback from two student editors.
- Once the revision forms are returned to the author, Krista emphasizes that students should treat the feedback as suggestions. She encourages them to consider the suggestions carefully, to determine whether they feel the changes will improve their piece. Authors will sometimes prefer not to make a suggested change; feedback from peers, and indeed from the teacher, needs to be evaluated, and the final decision rests with the author.
- Depending on the grade or the focus for the unit or assignment, Krista may address only one or two of meaning, style, or form in her rubrics, checklists, and peer revision forms. If all aspects are going to be evaluated, she will still often break up the peer revision to keep it as focused as possible. One revision mini-lesson may address meaning, and that will be all that student editors look for in their reading of the drafts. The following class, in different groups of three, student editors may focus their attention on style or form.

SAMPLE RUBRIC FOR A FREE VERSE POEM

Evaluation: Free Verse Poem	A good start. Spend some more time revising this piece.	A strong piece.	Wow!
Snapshot	*Attempts to develop a poetic statement with some literary devices (often rhyme or simile); may be contrived in parts*	*Creates a thoughtful poetic statement that features some effective literary devices and imagery*	*Engages the reader in a well-crafted poetic statement that features some powerful imagery and literary devices*
Meaning • insight • detail and support	• relatively predictable or narrow • some relevant detail	• thoughtful; deals with topic maturely • carefully chosen details	• interesting insights or perspectives • efficient, powerful use of detail

| Style
• poetic devices
• vocabulary | • poetic devices and imagery are often limited to simile, personification, rhyme; may seem contrived at times
• appropriate word choice; some visual description | • some effective poetic devices and imagery (a variety)
• some vitality and variety in language, with strong visual description | • original and inventive poetic devices and imagery
• effective and powerful word choices; may take risks, be playful |
|---|---|---|---|
| Form
• sequence, transitions
• line and stanza breaks
• ending | • clear sequence; lacks direction
• line and stanza breaks are logical but do not create effects or guide reader
• logical ending; may be obvious or may not offer closure | • clear sequence and direction
• tries to use line and stanza breaks for effect
• satisfying ending with a sense of closure | • sense of direction, building to a conclusion
• line and stanza breaks are effective
• ending has impact, leaving the reader with something to think about |
| Conventions
• punctuation
• grammar, spelling | • some errors in punctuation
• occasional errors | • punctuation is logical
• few errors, and these are minor | • may use dashes, ellipses, semicolons, and spaces for effect
• no errors |

Adapted from BC Writing Performance Standard

SAMPLE INDIVIDUAL REVISION CHECKLIST FOR FREE-VERSE POEM (EXCERPT)

Style

(Bullet one)

❏ Can you add more sensory detail; imagery, and figurative language? (e.g., change "I went into the kitchen to find some food" to "I raced into the kitchen and tore the fridge door open, ignoring my sister's latest preschool project and fridge magnets that flew to the ground")

❏ Is there a place where a metaphor would work well? Where alliteration would add meaning to your poem? Where other poetic devices would allow you to say more with less?

(Bullet two)

❏ Have you read your poem out loud to yourself a number of times, listening to your words and lines, underlining ones that don't fit with the rhythm of your poem and then editing these?

❏ Have you chosen strong, specific nouns and verbs? (e.g., change "He got dressed" to "He pulled on a mistake of an orange shirt and a pair of stained khakis") Have you circled your verbs ending in *-ing* and tested whether or not the present tense would be more powerful? (e.g., change "Dancing…" to "I dance…")?

❏ Have you cut any "really bad words" (*very, really, a lot, sort of, nice*)? Can you get rid of unnecessary adjectives and adverbs? Are there longer expressions that you can replace with shorter ones? Have you eliminated any cliches?

Form

(Bullet one)

❏ Are your ideas presented in an effective order?

(Bullet two)

❏ Have you thought carefully about where to stop one stanza and begin another?

❏ Have you thought carefully about where to stop each line and begin another?

(Bullet three)

❏ Did you stop at just the right moment? Should the ending be shortened?

❏ Does the ending leave the reader with something to think about?

❏ Does the ending have some "punch"?

PEER REVISION FORM FOR STYLE IN FREE VERSE POEM

Author: Editor:

1. Write your favorite image or use of figurative language and explain why you were drawn to it.
2. Can you suggest a place where the author might add more vivid sensory imagery and figurative language?
3. Read through the poem. Do you notice any problems with the rhythm of the poem?
4. Record a line that includes effective diction. What makes the author's word choice powerful?
5. Circle vague nouns and verbs. Circle verbs ending in –*ing*. Circle words like "very" and "really" and other unnecessary adjectives and adverbs. Circle any clichés.
6. Are there any longer phrases that you can suggest might be replaced with shorter ones?

Writing Workshops

In her creative writing class, Krista engages students in writing workshops two months into the year, after she's had some time to build a community of writers. This revision model requires a certain level of trust and maturity, as well as explicit modeling and monitoring, but she has also found that it is the most successful for her and her students. The discussions are often rich and leave the writer with specific direction and suggestions. They also help all students become more careful, thoughtful, purposeful readers.

Prior to this sequence, Krista works with her students to look at models of the genre, to pull criteria about what makes effective writing in that genre, and to compare that criteria to examples of student or teacher writing in that genre.

1. Krista begins by modeling the process with her own writing.
   - She passes out copies of a poem or short piece of prose she has written.
   - She projects her piece on the overhead and reads it out loud.
   - Students have three or four minutes to mark the text with their comments: passages they liked and suggestions for improvement.
2. Krista asks for a volunteer to begin the discussion of the piece, by saying something positive; aside from keeping a speaker's list, she herself says as little as possible.
   - Often students are hesitant to offer any criticism so, once a few people have shared observations that are complimentary in nature, Krista will ask specifically for constructive criticism. One brave soul will usually begin, and the discussion continues in a more balanced way.
   - The goal is for students to have a discussion of the piece "around" the author, referring to the author in the third person, and directing their comments to one another rather than to the author. Krista asks them to talk about the piece as though she wasn't there.
   - As students discuss the piece, Krista takes notes on the overhead, modeling how she records responses. When the discussion wanes, Krista shares the comments she felt were the most helpful. This is an opportunity to remind students that the more specific the comment, the better. "Your piece was really good" doesn't help an author improve. In addition, Krista shares with her students the changes she plans to make to the piece as a result of the discussion.
3. Next, Krista goes over the instructions for students, writing them on the board.
   - Students form groups of four or five, and number themselves off.

Students are told that in preparation for the revision process, they need to come to class with four or five copies of their draft. If they hand in their drafts the day before, Krista makes copies for them; otherwise, students are responsible for their own copies.

- Person 1 begins by passing out copies of her draft to the other members of the group.
- Person 1 reads his/her piece out loud. Persons 2–5 take three or four minutes to record their impressions and suggestions about the piece. It helps to write some prompts on the board:

  - What passage stayed with you? Which part did you find particularly powerful?
  - Was there a time when you were confused or when you felt that more detail would help?
  - Do you have specific suggestions with regard to diction or wordiness or sentence structure and variety? (Substitute questions that are relevant to the genre of the drafts and to the focus of the unit.)

- Person 2 begins the discussion with a positive comment. Persons 3–5 join in with their comments, and everyone discusses the piece as though the author is not there.
- Krista emphasizes these guidelines:

  - Keep the comments balanced. Be sure to provide the author with some positive comments as well as some constructive criticism.
  - Make your comments as specific as possible. Some concrete suggestions (what do you think about using a semicolon in the opening sentence as opposed to a comma and "but") are often welcome.
  - Treat all pieces as fiction unless the author chooses to tell you that the piece is autobiographical.

- When the group seems to have finished discussing the piece, Person 1 has the option to make a comment or to simply say thank you and collect all drafts.
- Person 2 then passes out his/her drafts and reads his piece aloud. Person 3 begins the discussion. And so on.

Writer's Circle

Krista participated in this type of writing circle as a university student in Professor Carl Leggo's class at the University of British Columbia. She has since adapted it to her English and writing classes.

While the writing circle works well during the writing process as a way for students to integrate feedback into their final drafts, it is also a lovely way to end the year. Students bring a favorite piece of writing to share, and the tone is one of celebration.

1. Students arrive at class with their drafts of a character sketch, a narrative poem, a descriptive paragraph, a personal essay—any kind of writing, although this works best with shorter pieces.
2. Students push all desks out of the way and arrange the chairs in a large circle or oval.
3. Students write their names on the board to create a speaker's list.
4. Person 1 reads his/her piece out loud. Person 2 comments on the piece, beginning with something positive, and continuing with other observations and practical suggestions.

Once students have had some practice with writing workshop and writing circles, revision becomes a natural part of the English classroom. Following a quickwrite, Krista will often provide a few minutes of sharing time. After a student reads a piece out loud, students chime in with specific comments of what they felt worked particularly well.

When Krista does this for the first time, and depending on the group, she may limit comments to positive ones and to connections (e.g., "That reminds me of…")

Krista never forces students to read their work aloud. They are allowed to pass, but everyone is expected to provide feedback to others. A few students may be willing to share their piece as long as someone else reads it for them.

- Having Person 2 responsible for beginning the feedback keeps that student focused on listening to the piece rather than fretting about his or her upcoming turn.

5. After Person 2 is finished, anyone else may offer a comment. Often two or three students will add an observation. Sometimes a piece sparks a lot of discussion.
   - Krista makes two or three comments for every student. This way, in addition to giving students immediate feedback, she continues to model how to make specific comments about writing.

6. Once no more comments are forthcoming from the class, Person 2 reads her or his piece aloud, and Person 3 begins with his or her observations.

7. This continues until everyone has shared his or her piece of writing.

Embracing New Literacies

When students walk into our classrooms, an odd transition/transformation occurs: they finish their cell-phone conversations, turn off their MP3 players, take off their headphones, and pull out their pencils and books. In some of the schools we work in, there are signs that say, "This is an electronics-free zone." When we think about this transition from being wired to unplugged, we realize that there is a disconnect between students' lives inside and outside the classroom.

One of the principles that we work from is to be responsive in our teaching, which requires us to build from the thinking and communication skills students already have and bring to their learning. When we shut them off from their most valued and comfortable ways of interacting and communicating with each other and the world, and only focus on teaching the skills of traditional literacies (print, paper, and sometimes film), we may discourage our students, dishonor who they are, and violate our principle of responsive teaching. No matter what people say about adolescents' levels of literacy, they are often deeply literate in ways that we are not aware of or do not utilize.

What our students are engaged in is thinking and communicating with what has been called "new literacies" (New London Group, 1996, 2006). So when we talk about this, what do we mean? Already, our definition of literacy is no longer limited to print media; we are working with an expanded definition of text that includes film, oral text, web-based media, art, dance, and more. With this expanded view of text comes a need for different thinking skills, particularly since many of the new texts are multimodal; i.e., include more than one type of media in one text.

Core Understandings: New Literacies

These core understandings guide us in our practice as we learn about and work with new literacies.

- We don't get to choose whether or not to address these literacies in our classrooms—they are now as essential as traditional print literature.
- Students bring with them a variety of experiences and comfort levels with various technologies.
- Technology is multimodal; that is, it includes more than one type of media in one text.
- We need to teach students multimodal literacy.
- Skills in new literacies need to be taught explicitly, as well as integrated into units of study.
- We need to use new literacies purposefully, not as "bells and whistles."
- It's important to examine the conventions of different forms of technology.

- We need to teach students to think critically and ethically about new literacies, because the public and the private intersect online.
- Because these technologies are emergent, teachers and students need to develop understandings of new literacies together.
- To be literate today means to be able to understand, integrate, and produce many forms of communication.
- Teachers need to advocate for equitable access to new literacies for all students.

New Literacies in the Classroom

We need to embrace technology—it's not a choice. It's embedded in our curriculum and in our students' way of knowing and being. The way our generation is TV- and movie-literate, our students are Twitter- and Facebook-literate. It can be uncomfortable and even humbling at times to not be the expert in the classroom, but it is also an opportunity to shift the way we teach: when we collaborate, co-create, and work beside our students, we are all richer for the experience.

In our initial conversations with each other, and when talking with our colleagues, the idea of integrating what we are calling "new literacies" brought up a few common responses. One response is to shut down as a result of discomfort and feeling overwhelmed by the constant change in communications technology. Another is to quickly embrace the latest media form simply as a replacement for print text (in a bait and switch). The third response is an interest in integrating new forms of literacy into teaching, coupled with a desire to ensure that we think through how they are of value to our students and fit with our learning goals.

In the end, we know that finding ways to teach with and for new literacies is responsive to who our students are, how they interact with the world, and what they will need to be able to do in the future. We're more aware than ever that we have to think differently about what literacy means today. We need to think differently about how people use and interact with technology, in particular how our students use technology now and will have to in the future. The fact is that we don't know what technology will be available in the future or how people will use it to communicate, but we do know that it will change, and that technology and the new literacies that come along with it will continue to change and challenge us. What students need are the thinking skills to use new literacies thoughtfully, creatively, and critically— and what better way to teach those essential skills than with engaging technology?

Our students have already developed many new thinking skills as a result of their daily contact with new forms of communication. How do we access and develop these skills to make them into better thinkers and communicators? This is the question we strive to answer as we try to reconnect students' lives outside of school with what is happening inside the classroom.

Examples from our Classrooms

The two units featured in this chapter demonstrate ways that teachers with varying levels of expertise and comfort with new literacies have integrated them into their teaching in authentic, meaningful ways for students. Our first example is a unit created by Leyton, Joanne, Krista, and Mehjabeen, in which students used technology to think deeply and critically about technology's impact on our lives. Then, Andrea Matza and Lisa Cooke share a global issues literature unit they co-created, which featured an online forum, linking students across the world.

Communications Technology Unit

We taught this unit as the first unit of the year in our English 11 classes. Although we planned it together, the unit looked slightly different in each of our classrooms, as we responded to our different groups of students. One of our approaches in the unit was to frontload how technology is key to English language arts; it's a primary way that we communicate now, and will be even more dominant in the future. We wanted our students to know that we welcomed the understandings that they brought about technology, but also that we wanted to help them to use it more productively and thoughtfully.

UNIT THEME

We began with a big question: *How does technology relate to what it means to be human?* By framing the unit with this big idea, we were able to connect across the themes for the whole year, as well as to get students to think about the impact technology has had and will continue to have on humanity.

ESSENTIAL QUESTIONS

- How does technology change/affect the way we communicate?
- How does the way we communicate change/affect the way we behave?

ENDURING UNDERSTANDINGS FOR UNIT

1. Text is a broad term that can encompass all forms of media, people, and art; we can apply similar strategies in our reading of each. (IRP)
2. Technology has significant impact, both positive and negative, on our ability to communicate with one another.
3. Language is a powerful social medium that we need to use responsibly and with care. (IRP)
4. We are shaped in a variety of ways by the language(s) we use.
5. Expression requires a form determined by purpose, medium, convention, and style. (IRP)
6. We need to reflect on, monitor, and regulate our own learning in order to improve. (IRP)

We had several skills, strategies, and processes we wanted students to develop through this unit:

- develop a personal voice
- connect and support key ideas
- express perspective or opinion
- use a revision process
- explain choices as creators
- determine the big ideas of texts
- analyze perspectives in texts
- engage with the ideas of others in respectful and meaningful ways

ASSESSMENT

The summative assessments we chose for this unit were based on our enduring understandings and on what we wanted students to be able to do:

We had some subquestions as well, which we thought about in the unit but which were not the focus of the assessments:

- How do we communicate with each other?
- How does communications technology humanize and/or dehumanize us?

Some of our enduring understandings were pulled from the British Columbia Integrated Resource Package (IRP) for English Language Arts 8 to 12 (2007: 2007), and some we brainstormed together.

- A personal essay on how communications technology affects me personally
- A self-reflection on learning, based on a series of metacognition-related journal entries

Setting the Stage with Big Ideas

1. Near the very beginning of the school year, we set up class blogs—after all, if we were going to ask students to think and view and write about communications technologies, we had better use some of them in our classrooms.
   - Mehjabeen set up a blog on blogspot.com for her students, and Krista and Joanne set up a joint blog on the same site for their classes.
   - Once we checked in with our administrators about any concerns they might have had around student privacy or safety, we were on our way.
   - We posted our welcomes and, once we began the unit, let our students know the web addresses for their respective blogs.

2. We spent the first few classes setting the overarching theme of the year, which was based on the question *What does it mean to be human?*
   - We had students solicit responses to it using some form of communications technology, including text messaging, instant messaging, e-mail, YouTube, and Facebook.
   - When students brought the responses they received back to class, we thought through how these responses were actually shaped by the form in which they were sent.
   - Once students had done some thinking activities on this topic, we had them write a diagnostic reflection on the question *How does technology affect our humanity?*
   - Throughout the unit, we tried to use as many forms of communications technology as possible in our presentation materials, formative assessment activities, student interactions, and student reflection activities. We also asked students to reflect on the technology they were using as they went through the unit.

3. We began to work with the idea of communications technology and its impact on our behavior.
   - Knowing that students were going to be writing a personal essay for the unit, we began by having students read an online excerpt of an essay by Paul Graham, "The Age of the Essay."
   - After an analysis of his ideas, students used what they learned to self-assess their reflective piece from the previous class—we were, in fact, beginning to get students familiar with the concept of metacognition.

4. The next class was a group activity in which students were given a slip of paper with a key invention on it, and they put them in what they thought was the chronological order of the inventions. This elicited some surprise as many students did not know how old some of the seemingly newer technologies actually are! After this activity, students selected what they thought were the top five inventions (of the list of 30 they had), and spent some time in small groups looking more deeply at a given set of inventions, responding to these questions:
   - What is the purpose of this invention?
   - What is one important impact of this technology?
   - How did this technology change the way we communicate?
   - How did this technology change the way we behave?

The blogs were open to anyone, but were set up as not being promoted or searchable.

This activity paved the way for students to begin work together on a model personal essay about communications technology and how it affects our behavior.

Leyton first used this activity with his Science and Technology class. By examining the impact of various technologies on society, we helped students infer the relationship between communication technologies and the way we live our lives. They were also able to understand how fast technology evolves and how we change along with it.

Feeding Students' Thinking

As a planning group, we decided that we wanted to model for our students the steps of writing a personal essay. We knew that many of our students were unfamiliar with this type of essay (they were more familiar with the "take a position and defend it" type of essay), and the kind of processes that might be involved in writing it.

1. We chose YouTube as the communication technology to be considered in the model essay.
   - As a way of introducing the students to the topic, we listened to an online broadcast of a Canadian Broadcasting Corporation (CBC) program called *The Age of Persuasion*. One episode, "The YouTube Revolution," was a perfect way to get students thinking about the impact of YouTube on advertising.
   - We prepared students to think about the personal essay topic by asking them a few questions:
     - What is YouTube? How does it work? Who owns it? What are some of the issues with it?
     - Who uses YouTube and for what purpose?
     - How often do you use it? Why? What do you watch?
   - Once we heard back from the groups, we clarified the features of the YouTube site, in case some students were not familiar with it (which turned out to be the case). We discussed how it differs from and is similar to TV, and the impact of the comments function. Then we watched three videos on YouTube and had students think about them as texts. We asked them:
     - What is this about? (summarize)
     - What is it trying to get at? (infer)
     - What is it trying to make you feel/think/do? (evaluate)
2. After each video, students discussed their answers as a group and as a whole class.
   - Then we came to our final discussion question for the class before beginning the essay: *How has this one communication technology impacted people's behavior?*
   - This was followed by a quickwrite to help capture students' thinking.
   - We also asked students post a reflection on the process of "writing on demand" on the class blog.

We discovered early in the unit that, when we used the blog for metacognitive thinking, it became a way to build community around thinking processes and struggles with learning.

Modeling the Process

1. We modeled the process of gathering ideas from our thinking and discussions in class, and asked the students to choose the most interesting ideas and explain why they were interesting.
   - Using Paul Graham's idea of "flow interesting," we wanted to start with some good ideas and let the essay flow from there, rather than having a set idea or point that students would be working toward. To that end, we asked students to post comments on the blog about what ideas they found most interesting from the class.
   - In the next class, we used the blog comments as our starting point in a mini-lesson on leads. We went directly to leads instead of the idea of a

thesis because we wanted students to see this essay as "writing to learn" instead of "writing what you learned."

- Together we listed, with students, good ideas for leads and then modeled a couple of examples, which students copied. We encouraged students to post on the blog some possible leads or directions the YouTube essay might take.

2. Over the next few classes, we modeled each step of the YouTube essay: possible leads; choosing one and making notes on possible next steps (see Model Lead); choosing one direction and developing it in a few opening paragraphs; mapping the rest of the essay (how it might "flow interesting") once a general direction was established.

- At each step, we showed students our own work, then had them try out their own ideas and share their thinking on the blog if they chose.
- We often pulled ideas from the blog to use in the next class.
- We did not model writing the full essay, but focused on modeling the process. For example, once we had a lead and a map of the essay, we went to endings and read some sample essays to analyze what makes a good ending; we modeled a couple of possible endings and asked students to decide which one was better and why.
- We also did mini-lessons on style, such as developing a voice or persona and looking at how the choices writers make influence their style.

MODEL LEAD WRITTEN BY TEACHER

Two years ago, I made the decision not to watch television—I have a nice flat-screen TV, but I don't have cable, and so it sits mostly silent and dark but for the occasional DVD. I felt very virtuous when I made my choice: no more wasted evenings flipping from one stupid, pointless show to another. Instead, I envisioned myself adding more quality activities in my life—reading, going for long walks, spending time with friends.

Alas, it was not to be.

Oh, I still don't watch TV. But the free time I supposedly created by not watching TV is being eaten up more and more by time in front of a computer screen. Granted, a lot of it has to do with my work. But I continue to have those moments when I glance at the clock in the corner of my monitor and berate myself that another hour has gone by and nothing has been accomplished.

Who or what is to blame for this?

I have to take some of the responsibility, of course. I'm the one who drags the mouse over to the Firefox icon on my dock; I'm the one who clicks on it. But once I've done the things I need or want to do, like checking my e-mail or reading a favorite blog, I am faced with a barrage of options that come to me whether I ask for them or not. It's impossible to ignore them—they stand out as links embedded in text, or they flash and whirl, trying to catch my eye, shouting, "Click me! Click me!"

SAMPLE BRAINSTORM OF NEXT STEPS

Where I might go next with my essay? (How can I make it flow in an interesting way as well as logically?)
- talk about some of the time-wasters online: humor sites, following link after link in a blog/comments, Stupid Videos, msn & celebrity gossip (even though I hate it I can't resist a peek sometimes), YouTube
- discuss how many of the other sites are relatively easy to get away from: they can be repetitive, are all on one topic (e.g., celebrity) → they get boring
- look at how YouTube is particularly addictive—how it uses certain features to keep you going: "More From"; bringing up related videos by topic/tag; also showing promoted videos; etc.
- give some general anecdotes of people's time being used up by YouTube and how much of a time-waster it is at work & home (may need to do some research?)
-OR-
- share an anecdote of how I have gotten trapped in the YouTube vortex and look at specific impacts YouTube has had on my own behavior

Weaving in Criteria, Feedback, and Metacognition

During the unit, students wrote meta-cognition journals on a variety of topics, including:

• How did our discussions and activities in class influence your writing/thinking today?
• How has the process of doing a practice essay affected your learning? What was most/least helpful?
• What is your usual process as a writer—in and/or out of school? What works for you as a writer and why?

See page 104 for the Prewriting Thinking graphic organizer; page 105 for the Final Reflection for Technology Unit.

1. When we completed modeling the process of writing a personal essay, students chose a communications technology to write about and used a graphic organizer to develop their thinking about it (see page 104). They worked their way through the process we had modeled and practiced together.
   • At this point we more explicitly reviewed the criteria for a personal essay and began to weave in some more metacognitive work by having students self-assess and peer-assess their work against the criteria.
   • Students' work was done in class exclusively to this point and we had been providing feedback throughout the writing process. Near the end of the process, after mini-lessons on revision and editing, we let students take their work home to polish it.
2. Before doing a final reflection on the unit (see page 105), students watched a YouTube video called "Shift Happens" which identifies the skills they will need in the future.
   • As a class, they reflected on which of the skills they have, which they need to develop, and how school or English language arts could play a role in developing them; students used these ideas as part of their unit reflection.
   • At the end of the term, which was partway into our next unit, students wrote a metacognition reflection on the whole term, which we used for summative marks.

SAMPLE METACOGNITION JOURNAL REFLECTION AND RUBRIC

This term, you completed 3 metacognition journals on the following topics:
1. How did our discussions and activities in class impact your writing/thinking today?
2. Choice of: A) How has the process of doing a practice essay affected your learning? What was most/least helpful? B) What is your usual process as a writer—in &/or out of school? What works for you as a writer and why?
3. Which of our class activities helped you think about and make sense of stories? How else do I think about and make sense of stories?

The task: a written reflection

Think back over the first term of this class and reflect on your learning. Specifically, you need to think about 3 big ideas in your writing:
• Who are you as a learner? How do you learn best?
• What are your strengths and challenges as a learner?
• What has been your growth, and what are your goals, as a learner?

Aspect	Approaching Expectations	Minimally Meeting Expectations	Meeting Expectations	Exceeding Expectations
Meaning • ideas • support • connection to learning *Value:* 8	• ideas are not developed; may jump from idea to idea • few supporting details, or mostly irrelevant • little or no connection to own learning	• ideas are clear and straightforward but unevenly developed • some supporting details are given • some general connections to learning	• ideas are developed fully and show depth in places • supporting details are relevant • connections to learning in class	• ideas are developed fully with some insight and maturity • supporting details are specific and telling • connections across learning situations

Aspect	Approaching Expectations	Minimally Meeting Expectations	Meeting Expectations	Exceeding Expectations
Form • organization • transitions *Value:* 4	• on topic but may seem illogical or random; may be off topic • disjointed ideas with few/no transitions	• states topic, develops ideas with little direction to a mechanical conclusion • awkward transitions	• establishes context and purpose, develops ideas to a logical conclusion • transitions connect ideas clearly	• establishes context and purpose, develops ideas to a satisfying or reflective conclusion • flows smoothly
Conventions • clarity • correctness Value: 4	• writing is not clear and is often hard to follow • many errors, often basic and repeated, interfere with meaning	• writing is generally clear but hard to follow at times • some errors (repeated, basic and/or distracting)	• writing is generally clear and easy to follow • some errors but they are not usually basic or distracting	• writing is very clear and enjoyable to read • any errors tend to be sophisti- cated; may take risks

Unit Reflection

- While not necessarily the most tech-savvy unit, this was, for us, a good first step into incorporating some of the technology that many students use on a regular basis—blogs and YouTube. The topic of communications technology also got students' attention and many of them were quite engaged in writing about things that are an essential part of their daily lives, such as cell phones, Facebook, instant messaging, and texting. Marking these essays gave us an opportunity to get to know our students—and a technology they use—a little better.

- We continued to build on students' engagement and facility with technology later in the second unit of the year (see Darkness unit in Chapter 8).

- We will continue to use new literacies and related technologies because they allow students so much more freedom in representing their thinking. We found that students' thinking was expanded and pushed in new directions when they read, viewed, and used new media and new literacies, and had to think about how the medium influences the message. As well, our own thinking was expanded and challenged—and on top of it all, we got to play with and learn about some amazing new programs and modes of literacy. Jumping onto the web to find a video, slide show, or podcast that explains or expands on something we're discussing in class is becoming second nature; the next step for us is to offer more opportunities for students to bring and use the technology they read, view, discuss and think about!

Global Interdependence: Online Literature Forum

Andrea Matza and Lisa Cooke worked closely as colleagues in Campbell River and then in neighbouring districts; when Andrea left for international school teaching, they wanted to continue this collaboration. They committed to the idea of connecting their classes through online literature circles. Andrea and Lisa wanted, through the application of new literacies, to help students realize that learning and school did not have to be isolated from their realities. They

In order to discuss and co-create activities, assignments, and assessment rubrics, they used Google Documents to develop their assignments, and Skype to discuss their ideas face to face. This enabled Lisa and Andrea to stay connected, and allowed them to co-create everything, often revising and commenting online at the same time—though one was at the end of her day, while the other was beginning hers. Students were given access to the unit documents by being invited as "viewers" on the various rubrics and assignment descriptions.

agreed that students needed to be involved in authentic conversations about real issues and wanted to provide a forum for students to talk to others beyond their classroom walls.

Connecting: Building Background and Interest

1. Andrea and Lisa introduce the unit with some activities and discussions that engage the students and build on their background knowledge. Additionally, they develop a variety of activities to prepare students for their online literature circles.
   - One such activity is a quotation gallery. Students select several quotations from Internet sources, such as Quotopia, record them on chart paper, and then circulate in small groups to post personal connections, comments, and responses to these ideas. After students walk through the gallery, the teachers have students brainstorm and discuss the benefits and drawbacks of globalization.
2. In order to encourage students to examine their role in the global community and to model the effective use of technology, Lisa and Andrea share two different video-based presentations with their students.
   - *The Story of Stuff* (http://www.storyofstuff.com) is an interesting animated video that Andrea picked up from one of her social networks. It allows the students to see just where all their "stuff" comes from, underlining the notion that, as members of a global village, our consumption can and does have ramifications in other parts of the world.
   - In addition to this video, Lisa shares a PowerPoint presentation she created called "Why Do We Have So Much Stuff?", pairing a collection of images and quotations about globalization, consumerism, and global concerns with Tracy Chapman's song "Mountains O' Things."
   - After showing these, the teachers ask students to choose one or some of the following questions and respond (by either supporting or countering the discussion point) with specific ideas, examples, and details using words and/or pictures to convey their ideas:
     - Do we (individuals, groups, North Americans, the global community, the more economically developed countries) have too much stuff?
     - Why do some (individuals, groups, specific cultures/nations, etc.) continue to acquire stuff?
     - Does this trend need to change? Why or why not? Explain.
     - If so, how can we effect this change?

Processing: Questioning, Analyzing, and Expressing

In the crunch to cover curriculum, students and teachers can miss opportunities to explore beyond the surface. Andrea and Lisa want to reduce the volume of content to something manageable and slow the rate of delivery in order to allow for deep learning and discussion, and thoughtful processing and reflection. Therefore, they are careful at the outset to keep the learning goals manageable.

1. To begin this phase, students write an impromptu response to one of a selection of quotations related to the question *What is my role in our world?* Below are some of the quotations used for this activity:

"In a consumer society there are inevitably two kinds of slaves: the prisoners of addiction and the prisoners of envy." Ivan Illich

"Our lives begin to end the day we become silent about things that matter." Martin Luther King Jr.

"You must be the change you wish to see in the world." Mahatma Ghandi

"In times of change, learners inherit the Earth, while the learned find themselves beautifully equipped to deal with a world that no longer exists." Eric Hoffer

"So now it is time for you to define your future, in this moment, through the greatness of your spirit and purpose." Kandra J. Gardner

- While Lisa formatively assesses students' work as impromptu writing, Andrea uses this impromptu response as a springboard to a multi-paragraph expository writing practice for her school's writing assessment. However, they both encourage students to refer to these ideas and to make further connections as they delve into their novels.

2. Andrea observes through her students' writing that idea generation and organization are weak.

- In order to support improvement in these areas, she has her students create mind maps to organize their thinking and to give them something to refer to as they move through the writing process.
- To facilitate mind mapping, Andrea uses another online tool called Mindomo (www.mindomo.com). There are several benefits to creating an online mind map. It allows the students to easily manipulate and move supporting ideas from one topic or area to another. Additionally, students are able to use color and icons, which helps to organize and clarify their thinking. By using an online version, as opposed to traditional paper and pencil, the students can more easily make changes to their work. Finally, because the software is web-based, students can easily access their work from home or school.

Online Literature Circles

The heart of the unit is the online literature circles, done through forum posts. Students engage in authentic conversations with students across the globe about the books they read.

1. To set up the online literature circle, Lisa and Andrea decide upon software known as Moodle (http://moodle.org) to run the forum posts for their online literature circles. Like the ones that appear throughout the World Wide Web, the forum allows members to create new "threads" for discussion on a variety of topics.

- In order to facilitate the process of communicating with people in a classroom in another country, students create a profile on the password-protected site. Through these, the teachers are able to contact students directly using Moodle, and students can read about each other.
- Students are required to post about their novel twice a week.
  - In each forum, Lisa and Andrea post the four essential questions. At one point during the three-week period, students must respond to each of these four questions.
  - Students also need to create two new threads for discussion and to participate in some of the discussions initiated by members of their literature circle groups.

Andrea had students get onto the Mindomo website and sign up for a free e-mail membership. As a class, they discussed central topics, supporting topics and examples, and how one would arrange these ideas. All that was required was an overview of how to use the software, and students got started generating ideas based on the impromptu responses they had already completed. Students also conducted student-led conferences for their teachers and parents. Many students chose to create a Mindomo map to organize and display their presentations for these conferences, citing its user-friendly and visual format as a great visual presentation organizer.

Popular titles, based on the number of forum posts, included *Iqbal*, *Breadwinner*, *House of the Scorpion*, *A Long Way Gone*, *Sold*, and *Three Cups of Tea*.

For more information about setting up Moodle for online literature circles, see Brownlie and Schnellert (2009).

Many people feel concern about unleashing groups of students online, worrying that some of the issues that emerge with online bullying and inappropriateness will surface within the forum. Andrea and Lisa went over guidelines for use with students prior to posting, including in their discussion issues of cultural sensitivity.

After hundreds of posts, they only once felt compelled to remove a post. This stemmed from a discussion on cloning, and both Andrea and Lisa felt that the comments were getting personal. Thus, they erred on the side of caution, conferred with the student, and deleted the student's post. That particular student then posted an apology for the other students to read. Otherwise, the discussions were often heartfelt, passionate, and educational.

See page 106 for the Online Response Criteria Rubric.

2. By having students engage in the authentic writing task of creating a biography to share online, the teachers were able to teach another short genre of writing.

   • Initially, they thought they would work through these post subtopics in a linear fashion, but the nature of an online community is not linear, particularly with 12-hour time differences. Lisa asks the students to respond to each question at least once and then frees up the students to choose where they post their other responses. This allows students to really delve into different issues on topics like the ethics of cloning, child slavery, and universal education for all the world's children regardless of gender.

   • In order to support student learning to create a quality post, Lisa and Andrea both write sample forum posts, projecting these for students to see and read, in addition to having paper copies available. They post these online in front of the students initially, showing students the process of adding a new thread to the discussion forum.

3. Instead of reading student work submitted in paper form, Andrea and Lisa read student work online. As a result, they are able to easily monitor the discussion board for any inappropriate use.

   • To support the content of the questions as students post for their peers, Lisa and Andrea present mini-lessons during class, using a variety of activities such as read-alouds with picture books, poetry and novel excerpts, Socratic seminar, and other in-class activities.

   • They share and discuss teacher/student examples for both the initial biography assignment and forum posts.

Assessment

Lisa and Andrea want to combine both formative and summative assessment for the unit. For the forum posts, they are specifically looking for improvement over time; to do this, they develop a response rubric (based on teacher Avi Luxembourg's North Island Distance Education School) for online posts (see page 106). Students are evaluated several times on a formative basis, then are required to submit a final discussion thread that is assessed summatively.

1. Using the "send a message" option on each student's profile page is an excellent way to provide immediate and paper-free feedback to students about their posts.

   • As the forum grows to almost 300 students, using options such as "complete activity report" and "participants" enables teachers to sort their way through the multitude of posts that appeared every day.

2. Andrea and Lisa are very impressed with the level of quality within the forum posts—not just in students' writing but also in their level of maturity and thoughtfulness.

   • Many, many students go far beyond the twice-a-week required responses, which leads to a higher level of authenticity. For any additional posts made, students are not assessed. They are participating at this point because they are intrinsically motivated to do so.

   • Many students who are relatively quiet in class are far more responsive and participatory within the forum. This format gives some students a "voice" that they normally do not have.

Transforming: Bringing It Together

In order to synthesize students' reading, thinking, and understanding, Lisa and Andrea create a variety of assignments that allow students to transform their ideas, especially in regard to theme.

- Students create mandalas as a way to represent their learning about character analysis and expression of the themes around the global issues books.
- Students have two separate analysis assignments—identifying and analyzing a theme in literature (all linked to global issues), and a global issues text study—in which they can show their understanding using a choice of different representations using technology, including PowerPoint, a sound/image recording through a voicethread, or a mixed-media presentation.

Unit Reflection

- After discussion, detailed planning, and reflection, Lisa and Andrea were reminded that they must continue to slow down and explicitly walk students through "what it looks like." More importantly, they were reminded how new literacies are "old hat" for this generation of learners. While many students need explicit details, discussion, and modeling before they can begin to analyze and respond to text, often they need little assistance with navigating a software program, especially a web-based one.
- Next time, Lisa and Andrea would like to involve their students in collaborative writing through web-based software, and would like to continue to find ways for their students to bring and integrate their own knowledge and technological expertise into the classroom.
- The theme of global issues naturally lends itself to use of the Internet. The fact that Andrea and Lisa relied completely on the web to create and conduct the unit meant that a greater emphasis was being placed on new literacies. Lisa and Andrea were also able to find and use web-based resources to further a concept, to emphasize a point, and to provide students with multiple modes for organizing their thinking, researching ideas, and creating representations. And, importantly, using the computer allowed them to collaborate, perhaps even more than they would have had they been teaching in the same school district, as they "ran into each other" online. It was this collaboration that resulted in a more richly developed unit.

One particularly powerful online tool is www.prezi.com, a "zooming presentations editor" that Harvard Business School calls "insanely great." It takes PowerPoint presentations to a higher level of quality and interaction.

By creating this thematic and topical unit, Andrea and Lisa were also able to work closely with others in their respective districts—teachers of humanities, teacher-librarians, and technology helping-teachers—which further enhanced the experience.

Communications Technology: Prewriting Thinking

The Basics

Name the CT you want to explore: _____

What is it, and what is its history?

Who typically uses it?

What do people use it for?

Beyond the Basics

What was life like before this CT existed or was widely used?

How did it improve people's lives? Does it have any negative consequences?

Making It Personal

How does or has this CT change(d) your behavior? Give specific examples.

How does or did it improve your life? Does it have any negative consequences?

Final Reflection for Technology Unit

To address the questions below, you can post the responses on our blog, post them on your own blog, e-mail them to me, or create a short PowerPoint presentation (1–2 slides per question) or visual on the computer and e-mail that to me. You may also create a YouTube video or podcast (if you know how) and send that to me.

1. List three new things you have learned/thought about since the beginning of this unit. These should be "Ideas" or "Insights," not facts. If there are facts that made you think of something, list the fact and explain what it made you think of. Explain one in more detail.

2. What are some the skills that we/you will need in the future? Think of two, describe them and explain why.

3. Do you feel that you have the skills that are needed to be successful in the future? Which ones do you need to develop?

4. How will/has English class help(ed) you to develop these skills?
   a) What have you learned about your own skills so far?
   b) What goals do you have for yourself?

ASPECT	0–5	5–6	7–8	9–10
• ideas and connections • metacognition	• Ideas and connections are not developed. • Little reflection, no goals are set.	• Ideas and connections are generally straightforward and clear; unevenly developed. • Student has reflected and set goals. May be very general.	• Ideas and connections are fully developed and show depth. • Student has reflected and set goals based on the reflection.	• Ideas and connections are fully developed with some originality, maturity, and individuality. • Student has reflected and set goals based on reflection. Reflection and goals connect to criteria/learning outcomes.
• use of Technology	Student has not used technology.	Student has used technology. Use of technology is at a developing level; some mistakes but they do not interfere with meaning.	Technology is used competently and effectively.	Technology enhances meaning and is used to advantage.

Online Response Criteria Rubric

ASPECT	Still Progressing	Minimally Meets Expectations	Meets Expectations	Exceeds Expectations
Position Statement/ Opening Question	Creates a discussion starter, but is not text-based. Does not include a personal position statement.	Creates at least one discussion question starter that is text-based. Includes a statement of your position on the topic.	Creates at least one discussion starter that is posed as a thoughtful text-based question. Provides a clear statement of your position on the topic.	Creates at least one discussion starter that is posed as a thoughtful and challenging text-based question. Provides a clear, strong statement of your position on the topic.
Depth of Understanding/ Making Connections	Your entry shows little understanding of the topic or issue at hand.	Your entry demonstrates some consideration or understanding of the issue.	Your entry demonstrates consideration and understanding of the topic/issue.	Your entry demonstrates a high level of consideration and understanding of the topic/issue.
Supporting Evidence • Opinions • Examples • Explanations	Evidence for this entry is limited or absent. No attempt is made to provide any examples, facts, or quotations to support the opinion.	Entry includes opinions, but may not demonstrate consideration of the topic or issue. It attempts to provide examples, facts, anecdotes, or quotations, but may not link to support the opinion. Evidence may lack relevance.	Entry includes somewhat detailed opinions that demonstrate consideration of the topic or global issue. Provides evidence, examples, facts, anecdotes, or quotations to support most opinions. Most evidence is specific and relevant.	Entry includes thoughtful and detailed opinions that demonstrate you have carefully considered the topic/ global issue to a great extent. Includes fully described evidence, examples, facts, stories and/or quotations to support every opinion. All of the evidence and examples are specific and relevant.
Responding to Others	While you respond to others' questions and responses, you do not build on the other person's response. Your response may demonstrate a lack of understanding and/or you may be impolite or disrespectful.	You respond to others' questions and responses; while you may not build on the other person's response, you demonstrate an understanding of what the other person was saying. You were polite in your response.	Responds to others' questions and responses; you build on the other person's ideas. Your response demonstrates that you understood what the other person was saying. You were polite and persuasive in your response.	Responds thoughtfully and thoroughly to others' questions and responses. Your response clearly demonstrates that you fully understood what the other person was saying, and you build on the other person's ideas. Whether you agreed or disagreed, you were respectful and very persuasive in your response.
Writing	Paragraph form is not used. None or few of the supporting structures of paragraphs are used (topic sentence, details/examples, concluding sentence.) Chat jargon and/or colloquialism is used and/or distracting.	Uses paragraph format; may include topic sentence. Examples and details are used to support, and may contain a concluding sentence. Chat jargon and colloquialism are rarely used.	Uses paragraph format (topic sentence, supporting sentences, examples and details to support, concluding sentence). Ideas flow and are clear. Although working in an online environment, chat jargon and colloquialism are not used.	Uses paragraph format (topic sentence, supporting sentences, examples and details to support, concluding sentence). Ideas flow and are clear. Although working in an online environment, chat jargon and colloquialism are not used.

CHAPTER 8

Constructing Critical Literacy

The four of us come from different contexts, and we are each a unique construction of the experiences and the resulting sense-making that we have been through. We engage our students in the construction of texts and of themselves, knowing that we, too, bring with us the perspectives and blind spots that we have acquired through the construction of our own identities.

To make sense of our role in this quest, it helps to start with a definition:

> Critical literacy is language use that questions the social constructions of the self. When we are critically literate, we examine our ongoing development, to reveal the subjective positions from which we make sense of the world and act in it. (Shor, 1996)

From our perspective, the question "Who am I?" can never be answered in isolation from the questions "What is my context? How do I read the world I live in?" and "How am I represented/perceived by others?" Understanding of self is tied to an understanding of the world we live in and of those around us. As students try to understand themselves, we hope to develop in them the tools to understand and work together with others.

Around us we see many texts—texts that are representations of ideas, beliefs, peoples, and perspectives. These texts try to persuade, convince, sell, and convert; all texts force us to think. Texts make up our environment, and our students are surrounded by these texts. As English teachers, it is part of our responsibility to work with students to develop in them the tools with which both to deconstruct the messages embedded in the texts around them and to become producers of texts that reflect who they are.

As English teachers we find ourselves in a position of opportunity as the core of our discipline is concerned with text, the site for so much identity construction as well as the repository of so many stereotypes. In stories, we find characters engaging in the same search for identity as our students. It is up to us to bring in the many diverse stories that are told in the world so that our students can understand how these stories have shaped the way people are represented, as well as find parts of themselves reflected in them.

Each of us struggles with the question "Who am I?" and our students, particularly as adolescents, are at the beginning of their search to develop their identities. Each experience that our students live contributes to this search. Students encounter many people, texts, and ideas and have experiences that help to form their response to this question. What is our role as English teachers in helping students to figure out who they are? What is our role in welcoming and supporting the development of each student's unique identity?

We have tried to develop tools of critical literacy by using cultural artifacts like written texts or media and having students examine the different readings of these texts. In this examination, we look at both how texts are constructed and how they are read.

In a classroom that aims to develop critical literacy, teachers and students must work together over time to develop the practices and awareness to uncover, share, and consider multiple perspectives. Students need to become aware of the structures they are part of and participate in:

> Critical literacy practices encourage students to discover how texts position them as readers and viewers and also to become more self-consciously aware about how their own textual practices work in the world to represent, position, and potentially silence others. (BC IRP: 20–21)

The aim of critical literacy includes the explicit goal of breaking down power structures that are embedded and perpetuated in language and representation. Creating a consciousness of how this is done is both the process and the goal of teaching for critical literacy.

Creating an environment where different perspectives and experiences are welcomed is key to the development of critical literacy. But we cannot stop there. Working with critical literacy is actually about being uncomfortable; it demands questioning and challenging self and others. In a classroom where critical literacy is valued, we want students to share, examine, and critique; we want to find ways to give voice to those who may be silenced in the dominant culture of the classroom. We need to be willing to share power and expertise with our students. This means figuring out how to identify power structures and understanding how they affect our construction of meaning, patterns of participation, and feelings of self-efficacy and agency. The end goal is not necessarily to come to consensus, but rather to come to a place of shared understanding that takes into account a diversity of perspectives. Critical literacy is messy.

Core Understandings: Critical Literacy

- Not only is the world socially and historically constructed, but so are people and the knowledge people possess. We create ourselves, therefore, with the cultural tools at hand.
- Texts influence our understanding of self, community, and the world.
- To capture and communicate our thinking, we represent it in text. When others interact with this text, they are interacting with the representation of our meaning.
- Power structures are embedded and perpetuated in language and representation. Developing critical literacy requires that students are able to see how language creates these power structures, as well as how it can be used to deconstruct them.
- We need to teach students how to interact with one another and texts in ways that are both respectful and critical.
- To access meaning, we begin from representation, to which we apply social, historical, cultural, contextual information in order to better flesh out our readings.
- Our cultural and historical backgrounds influence our point of view and therefore affect how we read texts.
- We all come from somewhere that is located in a particular historical time frame.
- Where we come from shapes our understanding of the world.

- In order to foster critical literacy, we need to create a welcoming environment in which students' background knowledge and prior experiences are valued.
- Critical thinkers consider points of view, examine bias, question the author's intent, and take into account context.
- An author's intention is not always what is written or read.
- When we read a text, we need to consider the author's background and perspective.
- We need to teach students how to look for multiple meanings in texts.

Many of the practices we describe in this book create opportunities for students to bring their backgrounds and previous experiences into the classroom. At the same time, we encourage students to examine and consider multiple perspectives. For example, using the structure of literature circles provides students with a range of texts with a diversity of perspectives and creates a space where students examine different perspectives with each other.

Many of the core understandings of critical literacy are also core to the literacy practices we outline in other chapters in this book. Central to critical literacy is the conscious participation in the construction and deconstruction of meaning, in positioning and being positioned by texts, and in the concern for how language wields and sustains power over others. While these ideas and concerns are quite complex and can often be relegated to the senior grades, we believe that they are important to all students and can be integrated into teaching at the younger grades. Building on a foundation of strong literacy practices allows us to develop thoughtful critical literacy understandings and practices.

Examples from our Classrooms

Below, you will find a junior and a senior example of units we have used to engage students in developing their understanding of, and practices related to, critical literacy. The first unit takes on some of the central concerns of critical literacy, such as the social construction of identity and how texts shape us and are shaped by our values. The second unit is a more integrated approach, as it aims to teach students the skills of construction and deconstruction of meaning within a particular theme that highlights the psychology embedded within and resulting from our forms of expression.

Junior Unit: Self and Other

This unit was developed by Mehjabeen, Krista, Leyton, and Rebeca Rubio for our English 8 classes. By the time students are engaged in this unit, they have already worked through at least one thematic unit and developed practices such as marking text, journal writing, literature-circle discussions, and group-participation skills. There is an established level of comfort in the class, both with each other and with the practices of considering big ideas and thinking together— this comfort is key to the success of this unit. In addition, the unit begins with short, engaging texts that foreground all the big ideas of the unit. Teachers work with students to develop in-depth understandings of the concepts of the unit with texts that they can all access before moving into texts that are more complex.

As students read through the various texts, they think about the way that each character's values are shaped by his/her own history and experiences. As perspective is a key idea being explored, strategies such as drama and writing in role help students to get inside characters and take on other's/their perspectives. Also central to this unit are the thinking strategies of inference and making connections: developing the ability to infer allows students to look more deeply into texts to uncover built-in assumptions and values; being able to make thoughtful connections allows them to connect the experiences of the characters they are reading about to themselves and to others in history and text. These thinking skills and strategies—core to effective literacy practice—are essential in the development of critical literacy.

ENDURING UNDERSTANDINGS FOR UNIT

1. We develop our sense of self (identity) through encounters.
2. Our individual histories make us unique and diverse.
3. People, ideas, and texts are connected; these connections are grounded in values, histories, and human experience.
4. To be able to articulate connections, we need to uncover these values and examine experiences.

ESSENTIAL QUESTIONS

• How does who you are develop through encounters with others?
• How does taking on others' perspectives shape how we see things/people?
• How do I build on or use what I know to make connections?
• What can I infer about a person's values by examining his/her life and history?
• How does text reveal perspective and values?

STRATEGY FOCUS

Drama and action strategies
Writing: Writing in Role, Personal Narrative, Writing with Evidence
Reading: Inference, Making Connections

ASSESSMENT

• Formative Assessment: reading journals, class discussions
• Summative Assessment: reading journals, novel project

Lesson 1: Introduction to the Unit

We start the unit with a short activity that introduces the main idea of Internal and External Perspectives.

1. Students are given a marshmallow and a Smarties candy. In journals, they describe each candy on the inside and the outside. They share their responses with each other.
2. We ask questions to engage discussion:
   • How are people like marshmallows/Smarties?
   • How do our insides and outsides differ?
   • Do we act differently when we are around others than when we're alone?
   • How many outsides do you have?
   • Do you give up parts of yourself when you are in different situations? Why do you?
   • Is it positive or negative that we change to meet the expectations of others?
3. We begin with our first short text that introduces the idea that how we see ourselves is often shaped by how others see us.

TEXT SET

Model Texts: Graphic Text/Picture Books
The Narrative of Frederick Douglass by Terry M. West
Something Else by Kathryn Cave

Model Texts: Short Stories
"The Fan Club," by Rona Maynard
"The Wrong Lunch Line" by Nicholasa Mohr
"Thank You M'am," by Langston Hughes

Model Texts: Movies
The Mighty
Mean Girls

Literature Circle Texts
The House of the Scorpion by Nancy Farmer
Waiting for the Rain by Sheila Gordon
Max the Mighty by Rodman Philbrick
The Sisterhood of the Traveling Pants by Anne Brashares
Define "Normal" by Julie Anne Peters
The Giver by Lois Lowry
Catalyst by Laure Halse Anderson
Shabanu: Daughter of the Wind by Suzanne Fisher Staples
The Old Brown Suitcase by Lillian Boraks-Nemetz
The Outsiders by S.E. Hinton

- We read aloud the picture book, *Something Else*. This book is about a creature who is not like anyone else and struggles to fit in.
- After reading the book aloud, we ask these questions: How does Something Else *know* he is "something else"? What role do others play in making him believe he is something else?
- We then ask students to make a personal connection by asking the question: Who are the others who shape who we are?
- Rebeca often ends the lesson with a quiet personal reflection on the following questions: Am I more a marshmallow or a Smartie? Who are the others that influence my life the most?

Lessons 2–3: "The Fan Club"

Our next set of lessons focuses on the second short text, a short story called "The Fan Club."

Found in Wilhelm (2002), "The Fan Club" is a drama activity used to build the thinking skill of inference. The premise is simple: by taking on other's perspectives through role play, we can get a better sense of what they are feeling and thinking in a particular situation.

1. We post the guiding questions for this part of the unit (pulled from our unit Essential Questions):
   - How often do we give up ourselves for others?
   - How does who you are develop through encounters with others?
   - How do we gain/lose as a result of our interactions with others?

Through these lessons, we follow the sequence in Wilhelm (2002).

2. Prereading: In Wilhelm's book, there is a "trigger" letter, a fictional letter from a parent to a principal stating that her daughter is being ostracized because she is "good"; the mother is worried that her daughter will give in to peer pressure and begin to misbehave/neglect her studies. We read the letter aloud and discuss it with the following questions:
   - What can the principal do/ who are the players here?
   - Who else needs a voice?
   - What does mom *not* know?
   - Is it true that kids get teased for being good students?
   - Are there different kinds of teasing?
   - How do you tell the difference?
   - When does teasing become harassment?
   - What "others" are shaping this girl's identity?
3. Reading the short story:
   - Students take a role (A or B).
   - Teacher reads story aloud, section by section.
   - At the end of each short section, teacher sets the role play:

   "A's, you are Laura; B's, you are an old friend from elementary school. You meet by chance at the mall. You begin to talk. B's, find out how Laura is feeling. Find out how she's liking high school, etc."

   - Students stand up and do the role play. They do this all at once; it is loud, noisy, unstructured.
   - Students sit and teacher does a quick once-around in the room, calling on students and asking them to speak in character:

   "Josh, what did you find out about Laura?" "Laura, who did you meet at the mall today?"

The goal is for students to become the characters.

- The class continues reading in this way, section by section. Each section students take on new roles. This activity helps students to engage with characters and also to understand the story.
- At the end teacher prompts discussion of motivation:

"A, you are Laura; B, you are Rachel. Laura, tell Rachel why you betrayed her. Rachel, tell Laura what you are feeling."

These conversations are interesting because students' interpretations of motivation ("insides") differ widely and set us up for valuable discussions.

4. Postreading: Class debrief of the story
- We go back to our initial guiding questions and the ideas from the trigger letter.
- We define monolog and each student is assigned a character.
- For homework, students write a brief monolog from the point of view of the character at the final moment of the story (when Laura betrays Rachel). It is important that the monolog reflect the facts of the story, the feelings/opinions of the character, and the voice of the character (through diction, vocabulary, etc.)
- Next day, students present their monologs orally: in their seats, they stand up and speak from their perspective:

"I am Laura. Today was the greatest day of my life—the cool kids finally let me in…"

"I am Steve. That was awful! It sounded funny when Terri described it to me, but now that the prank is done, I'm ashamed. I can't believe I let myself be sucked in by Terri's good looks…"

Lesson 4: Making Connections: Modeling

At this point in the unit, we introduce our next big thinking skill, making connections.

At this point in the unit we introduce our literature circle texts. Students are given a choice of novels. As we work through the short texts, we have them practice some of the skills that they are learning with their own novels: first by discussing the ideas in groups and then by writing about them in their journals. For example, after "The Fan Club" lesson, we might ask students to write from the perspective of one of their novel characters about a particular incident.

1. We begin by brainstorming the different types of connections with students (text–text, text–self, text–world).
- We work with students to develop criteria for good connections.
2. In small groups, students create their own connections for either "The Fan Club" or "Something Else."
- They share these connections with the class.
3. As a class, we develop a good connection related to "The Fan Club."
- We begin with "Rachel wears floral shirts. I know a girl who wears floral shirts," and work together to deepen the connection:

"Rachel wears floral shirts. I know a girl who wears floral shirts and both girls are discriminated against because they don't wear brand name clothing. They are both being judged by their exterior. Our society seems to discriminate against people who don't fit in to the 'accepted' rules…"

4. We have students make connections with their novels.
   - They meet in their literature circle to share their connections and they sort all of their connections into the categories: text–text, text–self, text–world.
   - As a group they write a journal entry about one of their connections on an overhead transparency.
   - Each of the groups shares their journal entry and we work together to develop the entries, based on the criteria we have brainstormed for good journal entries (see samples on pages 113 and 114). The criteria for a good connection journal entry might be the following:

     - The connection should have examples from the text.
     - The connection should have examples from world/self/other text.
     - The connection should be explained or "connected."
     - There should be a connection with a "big idea" or "value."

   - In addition, the entry should follow other general guidelines for good journal entries such as having sufficient and relevant detail.
5. Students continue to work on making connections throughout their unit, primarily working with their novels and writing journal entries.
   - They spend time in their literature circles discussing these connections, assessing their own and each other's entries, and bring the insights they develop into the larger class discussions that continue to focus on shared short texts.
   - With each of the short texts, we continue to make connections as a class, sometimes focusing on particular types of connections.

SAMPLE JOURNAL ENTRY 1

Novel: *The Giver* by Lois Lowry

Connection: Text to World

Original Entry by Group

In the story *The Giver*, the Eights to Twelves have to help the community by doing volunteer hours. In high school, Eights to Twelves also have to do service hours. In both worlds, we all try to help our own society and find our interests.

Examples from the text	✔	Suggestions to improve:
Examples from world	✔	Add more detail
Connection explained	✔	
Connected to a "big idea" or "value"	✔ Value = Service	
Enough detail		

Rewritten Entry

In the story *The Giver*, the Eights to Twelves have to help the community by doing volunteer hours. By doing this, they serve others and they also explore different jobs they could have. Jonas volunteers at the seniors' home and learns about what happens to people when they get old. In high school, grade eight– twelves also have to do service hours and also explore our interests. Many students find out what they are good at by volunteering such as members of the Natural club who may go into Environmental Studies at university. In both worlds, we all try to help our own society and find our interests.

Novel: *The House of the Scorpion* by Nancy Farmer

Connection: Text to World

Original Entry by Group

In the real world, they cloned sheep and in the book, they cloned El Patron. In the real world, cloning isn't legal but in the book it is. This is because people aren't ready for such a big step. In the book 29 of 30 clones die so its dangerous and any that were successful would be treated horribly. If they clone a person and it goes wrong, people would be angry. The government would be in a lot of trouble and would get sued by lot of people.

Examples from the text	✔	Suggestions to improve:
Examples from world	✔	• make big ideas obvious • use more specific examples
Connection explained	✔	
Connected to a "big idea" or "value"	Almost connected to a big idea Big ideas = cruelty, humanity (value)	
Enough detail		

Rewritten Entry

In the real world, a sheep has been cloned and in the book a person has been cloned, El Patron. In the real world, cloning people isn't legal but in the book it is because clones are not considered people, they are considered to be "livestock" or animals. That is why they can be used for organs or drugged and forced to work for the "real" people. In our world, many people see clones as people and don't want them exposed to the dangers of being a clone because they would be treated inhumanely.

In the real world, a sheep has been cloned and in the book a person has been cloned, El Patron. In the real world, cloning people isn't legal but in the book it is because clones are not considered people, they are considered to be "livestock" or animals. That is why they can be used for organs or drugged and forced to work for the "real" people. In our world, many people see clones as people and don't want them exposed to the dangers of being a clone because they would be treated inhumanely.

Lesson 5: Making Connections: Focusing on Text-to-Text Connections

1. Text–text connections are often the most difficult to do well. To deepen students' ability to make rich and thoughtful connections, Rebeca spends some time working with nonfiction text.
   - She assigns each group a nonfiction reading connected to their novel:
     - For the novel *The Outsiders*: a reading about a girl who leaves her gang, the inspiration for the movie, *Freedom Writers*
     - For the novel *Shabanu*: a reading about a growing up in Saudi Arabia
     - For the novel *Waiting for the Rain*: a reading about Nelson Mandela
     - For the novel *Define "Normal"* a reading about New York kids talking about finding your place in high school and in life

This lesson uses the thinking skill of making connections to build one of the big ideas of the unit, that context (historical, geographical, social, and political) plays a significant part in the development of our identities because it requires students to make explicit connections between the characters in their novels and their contexts.

- In their literature circles, students read the article and then, together, create text–text connections between their novel and the article.
- They select one of these and develop it further using the class-developed criteria.

Lessons 6–8: Using Connections to Understand a Character's Feelings

Sometimes students need more scaffolding or practice with making connections and with thinking through some of the big ideas of the unit.

1. We often stop at this point and watch a movie together, such as *The Mighty* or *Mean Girls,* and look at a short story such as "The Wrong Lunch Line" by Rona Maynard. Each of these texts shows how others play a significant role in shaping a person's identity.
- We have students watch the movie and make text–text connections as well as text–self connections.
- We have them work with one of our essential questions— e.g., How does the main character change as a result of his/her interactions with others?—and create a written response by the end of the movie.

Lesson 9: How Does our Background Shape our Values and Perspectives?

One of the key texts in this unit is a graphic version of a section of *The Narrative of Frederick Douglass.* Using this text, we are able to deeply explore the ideas that our values and perspectives are connected to our histories and backgrounds, that each of us is unique as a result of our unique backgrounds, that understanding other's perspectives requires us to learn about where they came from and why they have the perspectives and values that they do. While "The Narrative of Frederick Douglass" is a complex text, the graphic version makes it accessible and allows all students to engage with the ideas that are presented.

1. We begin this lesson by reviewing the terms "perspective" and "point of view."
- As a class we discuss the questions: What influences our perspective? What elements of our background shape our perspectives?
- We often have students create diagrams that explore these questions to ensure that students see how complex the possible responses are.

SAMPLE BRAINSTORM

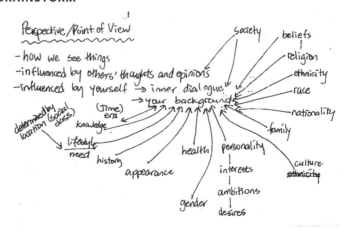

2. As a class we read the narrative.
   • We discuss what is meant by the term "values" by asking questions: What does Frederick Douglas value? What is important to him? Some of the responses our students come up with:

Freedom   Family
Education   His race
Equality

   • We ask students to list others who have been in his life and also the various parts of his background. We use the diagram as an organizer and have students complete a table.

SAMPLE ORGANIZER AND TABLE

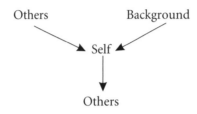

Frederick Douglass' Background	Frederick Douglass' Values	Others in his Life
• Where he comes from (southern US) • From Africa as a slave – culture and history of his people • Color of his skin (race) • Not taught to read • Social class – slavery is legal and he is a slave • Family – orphan, barely knew his mother • Personal ambitions and desires	• Freedom • Education • Equality • Family • His race	• His aunt, a mother figure • His masters • Aulds, Thomas • Covey • Plummer • Poor white children he meets • His wife, Anna • Newspaper, "The Liberator" • People who were fighting against slavery, "the north"

   • After they complete the table, we have students make connections between the various parts of the table to show how his background and the various others in his life shape his values and beliefs.

Lesson 10: Diagramming Influences

1. Building from the diagram created out of the brainstorm at the beginning of the previous lesson, we have students create more complex diagrams about how different influences shape us and what they think is most influential.
   • Students work in groups and develop these diagrams, visualizing and making decisions about what influences are more significant than others, and also representing the nature of each influence in some way.

SAMPLE DIAGRAMS

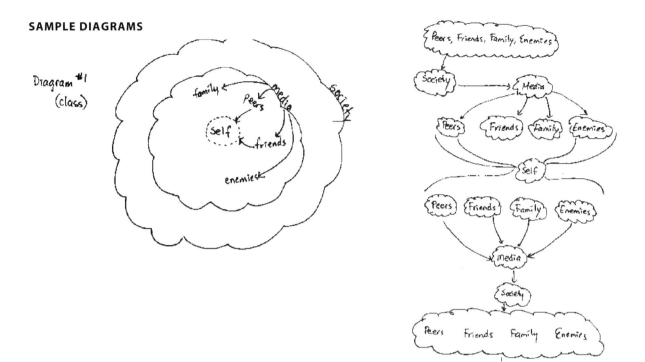

2. We have students work in their literature circle groups to list and develop diagrams that reflect the background and others in their characters' lives and how these have influenced their identity and values.

SAMPLE DIAGRAM

3. After completing this diagram, which can take up to a whole class, students write journal entries on one of these influences, selecting one of the most significant influences for their character.

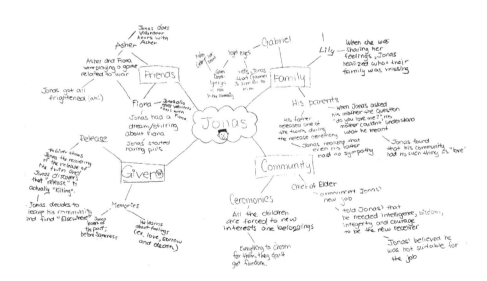

See page 131 for the marking rubric for this assignment.

Lesson 11: Summative Assessment

Our final summative assessment for this unit requires students to demonstrate their understanding of the ideas and thinking skills from this unit using their literature circle novels.

1. Describe at least 4 others that influence your character; include evidence from the text to show how.
2. Evaluate and explain which is the most influential and why.
3. Describe three important aspects of your character's background and his/her values. Create a graphic showing how the aspects of the character's background influence his/her values.
4. Imagine your character is in an alternate world and write his/her feelings/thoughts about the world, connecting this response to his/her background and values.
5. Write a paragraph connecting two of the texts we have studied in this unit.

Unit Reflection

- This unit takes on some of the ideas expressed in our core understandings for critical literacy. It explores the construction of identity as people are positioned by the ways that others see them, by how they are represented. It involves the taking on and consideration of multiple perspectives and shows how these perspectives themselves are shaped by a person's history, context, and encounters. It develops an understanding of the diversity of people's values and why these are unique and diverse. Finally, it develops empathy and insight without simplifying or reducing individuals into stereotypes.

- This unit is a long one; it takes time and many steps. The thinking skills of inference and making connections are essential in developing depth of insight in students; the rich and diverse texts are also key to the success of this unit. In the beginning, our students find this unit challenging but by the end they are themselves exited about what they have been able to do, understand and express.

- Ultimately, we hope to help our students develop the tools to become confident creators of themselves and be able to use language to express who they are and to think through who they will become. By breaking down the processes of identity construction we are able to help our students become aware of their own influences, to begin to think critically about their own perspectives, and to learn how to consider and understand the perspectives of others.

Senior Unit: The Darkness in Humanity

When we give students the opportunity to consciously deconstruct and construct texts, they have an opportunity to consider what language is used, how it is used, and the impact it will have on the messages being communicated.

Here, we outline a Grade 11 English unit on the darkness in humanity developed by the four of us. We deliberately chose a topic that is complex and ambiguous as this allows for play with language and ideas. We examine the language that is used within texts, how it is used, the assumptions and beliefs embedded within it, and how messages are constructed; we examine messages in all textual forms—visual, multimedia, informational, and literary. Part of this process is working with students to brainstorm multiple readings of various texts and how we come to those readings. Language becomes a lens through which we attempt to understand human motivation.

1. Our perceptions around evil, war, and violence are influenced by our contexts and experiences.
2. What we create is a representation of what we think and believe; our representations of meaning can be constructed consciously or unconsciously. Others can understand us only through our representations.
3. Expression requires a form determined by purpose, medium, convention, and style.
4. Language is a powerful social medium that we need to use responsibly and with care.
5. Meaning-making is a constructive and creative process; the quest for meaning is never complete.
6. An understanding of literature is key to an understanding of oneself, one's community, and the world.
7. The more you learn about a topic, the more you can engage with it and the more deeply you can learn about it.
8. The more you learn about something, the more you realize its complexity and how hard it is to come to firm conclusions.
9. Effective communicators choose and generate strategies depending on purpose and audience.
10. A good thinker uses interpretations, analysis, synthesis, and evaluation to deepen and enhance understanding.

ESSENTIAL QUESTIONS

While we usually try to limit our essential questions to three or four per unit, we brainstormed close to thirty for this unit, and could have continued. We decided on one main question and then created a list of subquestions that we focused on at various points in this extended unit, always trying to connect back to our overarching question.

Main Question: How can we make sense of the darkness in humanity?
Subquestions
- What do we mean by evil?
- Why do we always position good against evil? Why have we constructed this binary? Are good and evil opposites? What are the shades of gray?
- How do the choices we make influence our nature?
- How does the way we see the world influence the way we think about good and evil?
- What motivates people to do things we call evil?
- Is evil a habit?
- How do we live with (beside) evil? Do we fight it? What actions do we take?
- Why do many people not respond/react/take action against evil? Where do others find the courage to respond/react/take action against evil?
- What is our personal responsibility and social responsibility?
- How do the monsters in our art and literature reflect the darkness in our humanity?
- How do we represent evil in art/music? What is the role of art in helping us to make sense of evil?
- What disguises does evil wear?
- How do we deal with the darker impulses (the shadow) within ourselves?
- What is the relationship between the experience of pain and the experience of beauty?
- How are people who experience violence changed?
- How is violence a cycle?
- What is the particular nature of violence during a war, and what is the impact of this kind of violence on individuals and on societies?

- Close reading (marking text, identifying big ideas)
- Identifying and tracking symbols, images, and language (considering connotation, diction, figurative language, rhetorical devices)
- Mind-mapping and exploration of ideas using graphics
- Oral language from small-group discussion skills to oral presentation skills to listening skills
- Literary Response Essay Writing Process (making connections between texts, developing thesis statements)

ASSESSMENT

Formative Assessment: class and small-group discussions; oral presentation on a film; "evil" or "darkness" mind maps; quickwrites and responses; poetry response
Summative Assessment: three-word thinking assignment exploring the "meanings" of words (mind map, image, definition); small-group discussion (in literature circles); multimedia presentation; literary response paper

Lesson Openers

The theme for this unit is rich, and there are many layers to explore. We are able to broaden the scope of the unit with these openers, and students sometimes choose to explore a topic we introduce in this way in their multimedia presentation at the end of the unit.

Throughout the unit, we often begin lessons with quickwrites stemming from a prompt, short focused discussions, or a whole-class reading of a poem.

- We ask students to make connections between a piece of literature, article, or idea we look at briefly at the beginning of a class with texts we've examined more thoroughly, modeling and practicing the skills they'll need for their literary response paper that requires them to use multiple texts to support a thesis statement.

SAMPLE LESSON OPENERS

Quotations

"He who does not learn from history is doomed to repeat it." George Santayana

"As soon as war is looked upon as wicked, it will always have its fascination. When it is looked upon as vulgar, it will cease to be popular." Oscar Wilde

"Knowing your own darkness is the best method for dealing with the darknesses of other people." Carl Jung

"'Anything worth living for,' said Nately, 'is worth dying for.'
'And anything worth dying for,' answered the old man, 'is certainly worth living for.'" Joseph Heller, *Catch-22*

Poems: "The Man He Killed" by Thomas Hardy (students will often make connections with O'Flaherty's short story, "The Sniper"); "The Generals" by Shel Silverstein
Discussion topics: connected to the theme such as gossip or hazing or bullying; anything timely (a global conflict, something in our community that is in the news)
Children's books: *War* by Nikolai Popov
Songs: "Gassed Last Night" from the movie *Oh! What a Lovely War*; "Goodbye Earl" by the Dixie Chicks; "Sunday, Bloody Sunday" by U2; "Luka" by Suzanne Vega; "A Criminal Mind" by Gowan; "Goodnight Saigon" by Billy Joel
Paintings: Edvard Munch's "The Scream"; the clearcut mountainsides of Emily Carr

Lessons 1–4: Unit Introduction and Short Stories

1. We begin the unit with a quick brainstorm around our essential question: How do we make sense of the darkness in humanity?
- We explain to students that we will be looking at texts, having discussions, and doing work over the next few months that will help us to better answer this big question.
- We often frame our reading with one of the subquestions for our unit, and take the time to refer back to our essential question periodically, to see how our thinking may have changed.
- Although we may engage in different activities with each text, because we read so many texts during the unit we have students complete a simple graphic organizer to help them hold their thinking:

Text	Personal response	Specific activities for each text	How does this author convey the darkness in humanity?

Many stories are available online these days, and "Cask of Amontillado" is an excellent one to hear out loud. We like the version at http://www.loudlit.org/works/cask.htm.

- As we have students read each of the texts, we teach them how to mark the text for author's technique, such as imagery, rhetoric, figurative language, tone, narrative voice, descriptive detail, etc.
2. Usually, we begin by delving into two or three short stories. Below are some of the stories and examples of activities that highlight some of the practices of critical literacy.

SAMPLE ACTIVITIES

"The Destructors" by Graham Greene
- Students practice marking the text as we read "The Destructors" by Graham Greene. They also begin to complete the chart above. We focus on the following questions and students record their answers in the third column: *What is the context/ setting? Why do the kids destroy the house? What motivates this evil behavior? What are some parallels you can draw between this story and other stories, movies, TV shows, real events, etc.?*

"The Cask of Amontillado" by Edgar Allen Poe
- As this text uses some complex vocabulary, we give students a list of vocabulary and they write a two- or three-sentence prediction of what the story will be about, based on this list. They stand up and share their prediction with two other people in the room.
- We pause frequently and think aloud about our reading, encouraging students to mark their text and to read actively. As we're thinking aloud, we focus on the predicting strategy and on foreshadowing, irony, and the imagery, particularly in the final section of the story.
- Students complete their graphic organizer, with the following question for the third column: *Does Montresor believe his actions are evil?* It's important to discuss who Montresor is telling his story to in order to help students grapple with this question.

"The Killers" by Ernest Hemingway
- Some of the action strategies outlined Wilhelm (2002) and discussed earlier in this chapter work well with this story. There is so much dialog that we often use readers theater.

- In the third column, we ask these questions: *What motivates people to do evil things? How are people who experience violence changed?*

"The Lottery" by Shirley Jackson
- We consider foreshadowing, symbolism, irony, motivation.
- We compare it to "The Destructors." When Greene describes the boys' work, he notes, "They worked with the seriousness of creators—and destruction after all is a form of creation." We consider how this is true in both stories.

Other texts: "War" by Pirandello; "Just Lather, That's All" by Tellez; "The Sniper" by O'Flaherty; "Shooting an Elephant" by Orwell; "The Desensitization of 20th Century Man" by Cousins; sections of speeches by Churchill

3. Article on psychology: One of the big ideas we keep coming across has to do with context—why do people do evil things? There is a related question: Why do people sometimes not stand against evil? We consider this question by looking at an article on Kitty Genovese and the bystander effect.
   - Prereading: We brainstorm some reasons why people might not act against evil situations. Then we give students a concrete situation: someone is being clearly bullied/threatened in front of one or more people. Imagine "Chris" is an onlooker. How would he respond if
     – he were the only one present?
     – there was a small crowd looking on, but they were all neutral?
     – there was a small crowd looking on, some of whom were supporting the bully, some of whom were silent?
   - During reading: We read the first part of the Kitty Genovese article aloud to the class, and then ask: Why do you think the people in the apartment building did not act in the face of a blatantly evil action? Consider the ideas that were brainstormed during the prereading activity and add more.
   - The article we use discusses the Kitty Genovese incident and then outlines some studies psychologists did as a result of her murder. We pause before reading these results and ask students: *What other situations/circumstances might increase the odds of an individual helping someone in need? Think of five in your group and rank them. Share the top one with the class.*
   - Postreading: We ask students to connect the ideas in this article with the short story, "The Destructors." In particular, does it help them understand the boys' lack of action in response to T's plan? We also consider this quotation by Edmond Burke: "All that needs to happen for evil to occur is for good men to do nothing." Time permitting, we also discuss rescuers. Often one group of students will have done their oral presentation on the movies *Schindler's List* or *Hotel Rwanda*, so this gives us a starting place.
4. After looking at a few stories and perhaps an essay/article or speech, we pause and give students the following topic for a short response: *What ideas about darkness are you pondering?*
   - Because we play with so many ideas in this unit, we think it's important to have students record their thinking from time to time and to synthesize some of their ideas. This is the type of assignment we might also post to a class blog:

One of the most interesting things that can happen in a classroom is to hear the ideas and thinking of other people—to be amazed at how similar and different and reassuring and disquieting and stimulating those other perspectives can be. To help this happen in our classes, we choose and have students respond to one or two of the subquestions of our essential question: *How can we make sense of the darkness in humanity?* [List of the subquestions that appear at the beginning of this unit, with follow-up questions that clarify ideas for students.]

Lessons 5–8: Film Analysis

After looking at a few literary texts, we want to get our students thinking about the ideas in the unit using film. We begin by "reading" a film together in class. We've used a variety of films for this, including *Lord of the Flies, The Dark Knight, A Few Good Men,* and *Life Is Beautiful.*

1. We divide students into five small groups, and each group is assigned one of the following questions to consider as we watch the film. Because these questions can be challenging, we model how we might reframe the questions more specifically for the film we're watching together. The examples in parenthesis are for *A Few Good Men*:
   - What are the layers of context/setting in this film? (What is important to keep in mind as we think about the question of who or what is responsible for Santiago's death?)
   - How does the filmmaker convey darkness or evil? Is it through the plot, imagery, characters, setting? What expressions of darkness had the most impact on you and why?
   - Specific focus on character as representation of darkness: Who or what is evil in this film? From whose perspective or in what context? (Think about who or what Jessup thinks is in the wrong and why; who or what might Santiago's parents think is in the wrong and why.)
   - What factors contribute to this character's evil actions? What patterns in society or contexts help and/or hinder and/ or change their evil behavior? (What factors contribute to Dawson's actions? What patterns in society or contexts help and/or hinder and/or change his behavior?)
   - What are the roots of this person's choices/evil behavior? What are the choices he/she makes or could have made differently? (What could Markinson have done differently? What could Santiago have done differently? How might Jessup have gotten his way…without risking such terrible consequences?)
   - How does this character symbolize the darkness in all of us? In humanity?
2. We introduce their independent film task, or Popcorn Project. We explain the task briefly, and then model a presentation using the film we just finished watching together.

SAMPLE ASSIGNMENT: THE POPCORN PROJECT

Below you will find a list of feature films, all of which relate to the ideas in this unit. Choose one to watch with a partner. Any movie with a questionable rating should be rented and viewed only in consultation with your parents.

The Scarlet Letter	*Gangs of New York*	*No Country for Old Men*
The Corporation	*Life Is Beautiful*	*Fight Club*
The Last King of Scotland	*The Insider*	*Perfume*
Ironman	*American Gangster*	*The Color Purple*
Bowling for Columbine	*Dark Knight*	*Rabbit Proof Fence*
American History X	*Whale Talk*	*Hotel Rwanda*
Schindler's List	*Les Miserables*	*Shake Hands with the Devil*
Roger and Me	*There Will Be Blood*	*Mississippi Burning*

Cry the Beloved Country	*The Godfather*	*The Accused*
Through the Blue Lens	*GoodFellas*	*Lord of the Flies*
Erin Brockovich	*Apocalypse Now*	*The Magdalene Sisters*
Lord of the Rings	*A History of Violence*	*Band of Brothers*
Star Wars	*Michael Clayton*	*Oh! What a Lovely War*
Gattaca	*In the Name of the Father*	*Saving Private Ryan*
Kill Bill	*Dead Man Walking*	
Silence of the Lambs	*Monster*	

Develop a short (5 minute) oral presentation that includes

1. a synopsis – not too long
2. a discussion of one of the following questions:
   a) What are the layers of context/setting in this film?
   b) How does the filmmaker convey darkness or evil? Is it through the plot, imagery, characters, setting? What expressions of darkness had the most impact on you and why?
   c) How can a character represent darkness?.
3. connections to other texts (films, TV shows, songs, blogs, websites, novels, short stories, poems, articles…)

Lessons 9–10: Darkness Mind Map

1. Following a mini-lesson (often a review) on mind maps, students work in partners to create a mind map on darkness.
   • This is another way to get students to start to synthesize the ideas we've been looking at over the course of the unit. Following the film presentations, they have lots of material to work with.
   • We encourage students to use examples from the short stories we looked at near the beginning of the unit, as well as from poems or songs we may have looked at.
2. Students work on mind maps in class, and then we post them around the room.
   • We tape a blank piece of paper beside each mind map. Students do a gallery walk of the mind maps and, for at least five of them, they write down on the blank piece of paper one or two big ideas they got from the mind map, as well as the most interesting idea.

Lessons 11–12: Three-Word Thinking Activity

See page 132 for 3-Word Thinking Instructions and Rubric.

We want to encourage students to focus on language and the range of meaning that can be contained in words. The activities outlined in this lesson sequence have students focus on a few words that relate to the unit. In subsequent activities, we remind students to carefully consider how language is used. In order to allow students more time to complete the three parts of their three-word thinking assignment, and also to provide a context within which students can work with these ideas, we often have students doing literature circles (we've done these with novels and poetry); see page 132. In the classroom, however, these two lesson sequences run concurrently.

1. We begin by providing students with some background on connotation and denotation:

denotation is the part of a word's meaning that is neutral/factual information
connotation is the part of a word's meaning that shows personal preference or judgment (+/-, approval/disapproval); the connotation of a word is based on associations (memories, feelings, connections, attitudes) and often evokes the same in others; connotations vary by time, audience, and speaker; each person, family, cultural group, and society brings our own experiences and associations to words; some words have little or no connotation, in particular scientific and technical words; we need to be aware of the connotations of words we choose

- We then lead them through some short activities to begin to make them aware of the connotations of some of the words we often use (slim/skinny; woman/female/lady/gal/chick/sister/dame/damsel, etc.)
2. We hand out and explain the 3-Word Thinking assignment sheet (see 3-Word Thinking Instructions and Rubric on page 132) and then model the first activity, which is a mind map.

SAMPLE 3-WORD THINKING ASSIGNMENT

Word	Violence	Conflict	Pain	Darkness	Destruction
Denotation					
Connotation					
Questions to Consider	• Are there times when it is okay to kill? • When might violence be positive? • How much is violence nature or nurture? • What is the difference & relationship between physical & emotional violence? • What are different ways of experiencing violence? • What is the role of power in violence?	• What is the difference between basic, moderate, and extreme conflict? • When might conflict be positive? • How much is conflict nature or nurture? • What types of conflict are there and how are they similar & different? (physical, emotional, cultural, intellectual, etc.) • What are different ways of experiencing conflict? • What is the role of power in conflict?	• When might pain be positive? • Is it possible to avoid pain? Should we want to? • Is pain necessary for growth? • What is the difference & relationship between physical and emotional pain? • What are the different ways of experiencing pain? Of inflicting pain? Of dealing with pain?	• What are the ways darkness manifests itself in the world? (e.g., anger, addictions, isolation, depression, abuse) How do people respond to or deal with their dark impulses? • When might darkness be positive? • What are some beliefs about darkness in humanity? • What is the difference & relationship between darkness & pain? • Is experiencing & dealing with individual &/or social darkness necessary for growth?	• When might destruction be positive? • Is it possible to avoid destruction? Should we want to? • Is destruction necessary for growth? • What is the difference & relationship between destruction & violence? • What are some things that might be destroyed and what might be the impact of that destruction? • What is the role of power in destruction?

3. Mind Map: We model each of the three assignments using the word *blood*. Students completed a mind map on *darkness* earlier in the unit, so we debrief this before beginning.
   - Students work in pairs for a few minutes on a *blood* mind map.

- We pool ideas on the board and consider together how best to organize and connect ideas.
- We use this class model to discuss the criteria for the mind map on their assignment sheet.
- Students then begin to work on their own mind maps.
- We use a similar process for all three parts of the three-word assignment (mind map, image, definition):
  1. Teacher models by completing the assignment for the word *blood* with the students and applying the criteria to this assignment.
  2. Students have a few minutes to brainstorm and share ideas with their small groups at the end of a period.
  3. They come to class the following day with a draft which they share in groups. They give peer feedback using the criteria.
  4. Students revise based on feedback and criteria.

4. Image
  - We use a similar process for the image:
    1. Teacher models by completing the assignment for the word *blood* with the students and applying the criteria to this assignment.
    2. Students have a few minutes to brainstorm and share ideas with their small groups at the end of a period.
    3. They come to class the following day with a draft which they share in groups. They give peer feedback using the criteria.
    4. Students revise based on feedback and criteria.

5. Definition
  - We use a similar process for the definition:
    1. Teacher models by completing the assignment for the word *blood* with the students and applying the criteria to this assignment.
    2. Students have a few minutes to brainstorm and share ideas with their small groups at the end of a period.
    3. They come to class the following day with a draft which they share in groups. They give peer feedback using the criteria.
    4. Students revise based on feedback and criteria.

Lesson 14: Presentation

Once students have been exposed to and begun to play with terms such as "connotation" and "denotation," and the ways that images influence our thinking, we try to push this thinking further by turning these lenses onto more familiar ideas and texts from the world around them. We hope to have students realize that even within these are embedded values and ideologies.

1. Mehjabeen put together a short presentation that explores the word "war" and how its connotation has changed over time.
   - The presentation looks at what war meant before World War I and how this meaning was created through rhetoric, literature, war posters, and language.
   - She uses the images from the war and juxtaposes them with words with positive connotation (*glory, patriotism, perseverance, preparation, passion, dedication, mercy, power, authority, beauty, remembrance*) to show how the combination of an image and word can create a "meaning" that is new.

- She then leads students through an examination of poetry from WWI and shows them the photographs of war that tell a different story from the war posters and rhetoric.
- She uses the same images and juxtaposes a couple with different words with a more realistic or negative connotation. She asks students to select the words to match the images in order to have them construct their own meanings and beliefs about war.

Lessons 15–22: Literature Circles

We've done different things at this point in the unit. What's important is to have students discussing texts together, focusing on language and on how language affects the meaning of these texts.

1. POETRY

We begin with a think-aloud with a poem that relates to our theme, such as "Five Ways to Kill a Man" by Edwin Brock.

- We use an overhead to show our thinking process and to make our marking of the text visible to our students. We focus on word choices and meanings/connotations of words because we want students to bring this focus to their own work.
- We then invite students to respond to a poem in some way. We might have students do a choral reading or a version of a verbal-visual essay.
- To prepare for a multimedia response, we give students the choice of three poems: "Luka" by Suzanne Vega, "The Baker" by Heather Cadsby, and "Dulce et Decorum Est" by Wilfred Owen. Students worked with a partner to read, discuss, and mark the text of their poem, focusing on word choices. Students record their own reading of the poem and then synch this with images and other sounds to create a multimedia response. Some students upload digital photos and others take photographs in combination with images from the Internet. Students have two periods to work on this, and then we project each video and discuss the choices the creators made.
- Regardless of the form of the response (choral reading, visual representation, multimedia), we limit the number of poems to three so that students can see how different pairs interpret the same poem. This gives them a visual representation of multiple readings of texts. In the case of the multimedia responses, it also shows how seeing different images can alter one's understanding of a poem.
- After the work with close readings of poems, we begin literature circles using poems; see detailed outline of process in Chapter 4; see also the section on Poetry Literature Circles on page 47. We used the following poems in our text sets:

Joanne and Krista had the good fortune of a month's use of our district's portable iMac lab. Some students had worked with iMovie before, but some hadn't, so the direct instruction and follow-up tech support of Gordon Powell, our district technology consultant, was extremely helpful. Because we did this work with iMovie, some students, who wouldn't have otherwise, used this technology to complete the major multimedia presentation outlined later in the unit.

Topic	Set 1: Medium	Set 2: Challenging	Set 3: Medium	Set 4: Challenging	Set 5: Challenging
War	"The Man He Killed" Thomas Hardy	"Hiroshima Exit" Joy Kogawa	"Ten Days Leave" W.D. Snodgrass	"Do Not Weep, Maiden, For War is Kind" Stephen Crane	"What Do I Remem- ber of the Evacua- tion" Joy Kogawa
Abuse/ control/ prejudice	"The Execution" Alden Nowlan	"The Immig- rants" Margaret Atwood	"Hard Rock Returns to Prison from the Hospital for the Criminal Insane" Etheridge Knight	"A Work of Artifice" Marge Piercy	"My Last Duchess" Robert Browning
Violence/ media	"Ballad of Birming- ham" Dudley Randall	"Out, Out—" Robert Frost	"What's Wrong with This Picture" Maxine Tynes	"Musée des Beaux Arts" W.H. Auden	"Sonnet" Anne Clifford
Other	"The Poison Tree" William Blake	"The Addict" Anne Sexton	"I Am A Rock" Paul Simon	"The Bull Moose" Alden Nowlan	"History Lesson" Jeannette C. Armstrong

2. NOVELS

Different combinations of the following novels work well for literature circle sets depending on the focus (war, darkness, evil):

All Quiet on the Western Front by Erich Maria Remarque
The Wars by Timothy Findley
Obasan by Joy Kogawa
Snow Falling on Cedars by David Guterson
Lord of the Flies by William Golding
Maus I and II by Art Spiegelman
Ghost Soldiers by Hampton Sides
B for Buster by Iain Lawrence
Private Peaceful by Michael Morpurgo
The Lovely Bones by Alice Sebold
Catch-22 by Joseph Heller
The Kite Runner by Khaled Hosseini
The Picture of Dorian Gray by Oscar Wilde
Night by Elie Wiesel

- Students read these novels in groups and mark the text looking for imagery, symbol, language, and other techniques that create meaning. Rather than focusing on the plot of each novel, Mehjabeen asks students to pull out the images, words, and quotations that are most powerful in the novel.
- She then has students keep a list of these and work with them to uncover what effects these have on them and what meaning is conveyed in them.

- Often the novels in this unit are not written in a linear style or are full of imagery, and students learn that meaning is primarily conveyed through imagery, symbol, mood, and language.
- At the end of the unit, students write an essay on their novel, focusing on these techniques and how they relate to the theme of darkness.

Lesson 23: Assigning Multimedia Presentations

See page 133 for Multimedia Presentation Rubric.

The major unit project is a multimedia presentation in which students explore an area of interest within the broad theme of the unit, and create a presentation using the various techniques that they have been deconstructing and exploring.

- They create a thesis that represents their ideas about a topic and construct a text that conveys this. They also "read" each other's texts and provide responses to each other's ideas and perspectives.
- We give students three to four periods or part-periods to work on this in class.
- We spend a lot of time, particularly in the first two working periods, conferencing with students about their topics and helping them to focus or flesh out their ideas. Students come up with powerful and varied presentations.
- See page 131 for the assignment sheet; page 133 for the rubric. The audience response we use during the presentations themselves can be found in Chapter 4 on Oral Language.

SAMPLE ENGLISH 11 MULTIMEDIA PRESENTATION

In order to get more deeply into our investigation of the question "How do we make sense of the darkness in humanity?" I invite you to develop a multimedia presentation that explores a theme, question, or idea about evil/darkness.

To express your understandings and ideas, create a multimedia presentation that shows your thinking and draws the audience into your thinking. Your presentation should be a response to some of the ideas that we have been exploring in this unit.

You can develop your presentation in a variety of ways:

1. Select a question (or 2 or 3) from the class blog [list the subquestions for the unit] and respond to or explore it (you don't have to find THE answer). Or generate your own inquiry question to explore.
2. Develop a thesis about the topic and have your presentation prove it.
3. Develop a piece of art (story, film, dance, song, etc.) that synthesizes your idea(s) and explains it/them—both perform/show your piece and explain it to the audience.
4. Find a belief about evil/darkness (your own or others') and investigate why people believe it; present the belief and your opinion about it to the class.
5. Take a quote about darkness and develop a presentation explaining/exploring what it means (seek quotations from literature, online sources, or books of quotations). An example from *Tomorrow, When the War Began*:

   "Humans had created these opposites: Nature recognized no opposites." (page 211)
   "So, that was Nature's way. The mosquito felt pain and panic but the dragonfly knew nothing of cruelty. He didn't have the imagination to put himself in the mosquito's place. He just enjoyed his meal. Humans would call it evil, the big dragonfly destroying the mosquito and ignoring the little insect's suffering. Yet humans hated mosquitoes too, calling them vicious and bloodthirsty. All these words, words like "evil" and "vicious", they meant nothing to Nature. Yes, evil was a human invention." (page 236)

6. Develop your own—get your idea checked by me.

Some important guidelines:

- You can work alone or in a group of up to four people.
- Your presentation must have a thesis (like in an essay) but you do not have to state it explicitly.
- You must use some form of media, art, or technology in your presentation (do not write an essay, and do not only speak/give a speech).
- You will present in front of the whole class.
- You will get some time on _____ to work on this assignment. **Presentations will be on** _____.

Lessons 24–30: Multimedia Presentation Work and Class Presentations

1. We find that three work periods in a row are often not effective. Class time isn't always well spent.
   - We often give students one period to begin thinking, and then teach a lesson on indifference using Elie Wiesel's speech "The Perils of Indifference" and Ursula LeGuin's short story "The Ones Who Walk Away from Omelas" before giving them one or two more periods to work on their presentation.
   - We might also take 15–20 minutes at the beginning of a student work period to look at a story, essay, poem, or article we didn't get to that we feel would enrich the work students are doing.
2. The unit culminates with the class presentations and the discussions that follow.
   - In Mehjabeen's class, she has had students read novels exploring darkness and how it is conveyed through imagery and language. Krista and Joanne have their students write an essay on one of the subquestions about darkness and teach students how to reference a variety of literary texts to support their thinking.

Unit Reflection

- By the end of this long and rich unit, students have become immersed in language, its techniques, its meanings, its conventions. They have deconstructed and constructed meanings and expressions, and they have engaged in many discussions exploring their own and others' perspectives.
- Following this unit, we find that they have learned to read and uncover meaning in ways that are highly sophisticated and that they now bring to all the texts that they encounter.

Marking Rubric for Novel Assignment

Aspects	You can do it. Spend some extra time with the criteria and ask for help.	Good start. Your engine is revving.	You did it.	Great Work!
PART A Explanation of how each "other" influences your character. Reasons and quotes to support the above explanations	• not a lot of thinking is evident; may be illogical in places • little or no support (few details/examples)	• straightforward thinking; may be simple and obvious, but is logical • some examples and some detail	• thinking is clear and logical; some insight • reasons and examples support all opinions and are developed with detail	• thinking is logical and insightful; some complexity • specific, relevant detail; variety of well-developed examples
PART B Understanding of background of character and how it influences his/her values (Table and Monolog)	• is not able to identify aspects of background or values • does not share the feelings, opinions, and ideas of the character • perspective seems the same or nearly the same as the original • character is not believable	• lists aspects of background and values, connections are not clear • reflects some of the feelings, opinions, and ideas of the character • reflects a perspective somewhat different from the original • character is loosely developed and somewhat believable	• lists aspects of background and values, some connections evident • accurately reflects the feelings, opinions, and ideas of the character • character is mostly believable	• connects background and values • accurately reflects the feelings, opinions, and ideas of the character • provides some insight into the character or a "new perspective" from the original text • character is fully believable
PART C Graphic	• image is very basic; little thinking is evident; may not refer to others or to background	• image includes references to others, aspects of back-ground, and perhaps how they influence the self • connections are not developed	• image includes references to others, aspects of back-ground, and how they influence the self • ideas are connected.	• image includes references to others, aspects of background, and how they influence the self • thinking is insightful and deep
PART D Connections	• very little thinking is evident; may not make sense or be kind of "random"; • few or no examples • little or no detail	• thinking is simple and makes sense; points may be very obvious • some examples • some detail	• thinking is clear and logical, may have some depth • straightforward points • points have reasons or examples • points are developed with detail	• thinking is logical, thought-out, and insightful • may have some unusual points but in a thoughtful way • points have good reasons and examples • points are developed with good, specific detail; may also have variety in detail/examples
Overall (presentation, conventions, organization, identification of most significant idea)	• lack of effort in terms of presentation and/or conventions	• satisfactory work; may be concerns about presentation or conventions	• very good effort; completed with care	• outstanding effort; completed with extra care

3-Word Thinking Instructions and Rubrics

1. For each of the 3 words you chose, brainstorm and develop definitions/explanations that take into consideration their denotation, their connotation, and as many of the questions as possible.
2. For one of the words, create a mind map of the term that defines/explains/explores the word as well as gives examples of it.

Mind Map Rubric	Minimally Meets Expectations	Fully Meets Expectations	Exceeds Expectations
• Understanding of word (denotation & connotation) • Organization of map (central image, use of color/codes/links)	• mind map conveys a basic understanding of the word, with some associations and examples • central image is present but literal or limited, several connections between ideas are made but are not always clear	• mind map conveys a thorough understanding of the word, with several associations & examples • central image is meaningful; many connections between ideas are made & are clear	• mind map conveys an insightful understanding of the word, with rich multiple associations & examples • central image is metaphorical; many connections between ideas are made & are clear

3. For another one of the words, create an original image or symbol, or a collage that defines/explains/ explores the word. Provide a brief written explanation (bullets/charts/paragraph is fine) of the thinking behind the image.

Image Rubric	Minimally Meets Expectations	Fully Meets Expectations	Exceeds Expectations
• Understanding of word (denotation & connotation)	• image(s) convey(s) a basic understanding of the word, with some associations and examples	• image(s) convey(s) a thorough understanding of the word, with several associations & examples	• image(s) convey(s) an insightful understanding of the word, with rich multiple associations & examples

4. For the third word, write a 300–500-word definition/explanation/exploration of the word. Staple your draft to the good copy.

Writing Rubric	Minimally Meets Expectations	Fully Meets Expectations	Exceeds Expectations
• Understanding of word (denotation & connotation)	• writing conveys a basic understanding of the word • some relevant supporting details & examples; may be vague at times	• writing conveys a thorough understanding of the word, with associations • supporting details & examples are relevant and clear	• writing conveys an insightful understanding of the word, with rich multiple associations • details & examples are specific, effective & may show subtlety
• Style (sentence length and types; use of punctuation for effect; strong nouns & verbs; concise & precise word choice; similes, metaphors, etc.)	• writing is clear; attempts to engage the reader but is awkward at times • attempts to use some techniques for effect (sentence structure, diction, figurative language)	• writing attempts to engage the reader and is occasionally successful • uses some techniques for effect (sentence structure, diction, figurative language)	• writing is engaging throughout • uses a variety of effective techniques (sentence structure, diction, figurative language); takes some risks with writing style (these attempts may not be as effective)

Grading Scale: I C- C C+ / B- B B+ / A- A A+

Multimedia Presentation Rubric

Topic:	Group members:

	Must redo!	C	B	A
Organization • beginning-middle-end • transitions	• introduction is missing or weak; conclusion is weak or omitted • presentation is not organized and/or is illogical	• has a basic beginning, middle, and end • transitions are present but awkward at times	• introduction is clear and sets up the presentation; conclusion provides closure • presentation is clear and uses good transitions	• introduction is engaging; ending provides a "so what" for audience • presentation flows smoothly and is easy to understand
Content • main ideas • supporting details	• content is sparse, vague or incomplete • no clear "main" idea or thesis • supporting details are irrelevant	• content is researched but is fairly general • main idea is supported, but needs more depth in thinking or in supporting details	• content is researched and thought-out • main idea is supported and developed with some depth	• content is relevant, significant, thoughtful, and interesting • main idea is developed insightfully and is well-supported
Media, Art, and Technology (visuals, audio, props, etc.)	• MAT do little to support ideas, may be distracting or go on for too long	• MAT are related to content but could be used more effectively	• MAT are related to the main idea and help to make presenters' point	• MAT are clear and interesting; they enhance meaning and are very effective
Delivery • clarity • engagement • preparation and practice	• presentation is difficult to follow • presenters make little attempt to engage audience, or turn audience off the presentation • little preparation or practice is evident either individually or as a group; presenters stumble and consult each other often	• presentation is somewhat clear, but parts are hard to follow • presenters use limited techniques to engage audience at times (e.g., introduction) • presenters are prepared individually but not as a group; presenters pause often, consult notes to explain points; need practice	• presentation is clear and easy to follow • presenters use good techniques to engage audience throughout the presentation • presenters are prepared both individually and as a group; there are few awkward moments; it is evident the presenters have practiced	• presentation is clear and well-articulated • presenters use a variety of often-sophisticated techniques to engage audience throughout the presentation • presenters are prepared both individually and as a group; there are only minor awkward moments; presenters know their stuff

CHAPTER 9

Integrating Content Areas

A unit based on the question *What is evil?* (see Chapter 8) allows us to delve into psychology, criminology, and philosophy.

We can all recall teaching experiences where we felt like our students were really engaged and where there was deep learning going on. In many of these instances, students feel that they have learned something about the world and how it works. In the previous chapters of this book you have read about ways that we integrate the different strands of language arts within a single thematic unit. This integration has caused us to teach fewer units within a school year, but to teach units within which students develop strategies and understandings that cut across reading, writing, speaking, viewing, listening, and representing. Thematic units also help us to look to other disciplines. When teaching ELA in a secondary school, it is easy to draw from topics and themes from the social studies and science curricula.

Another way to develop units that promote and sustain deep learning that feels relevant for students is to integrate subject areas within a unit. This involves actually braiding together two or more curricula within a single thematic unit—addressing learning outcomes from each. All three scenarios—linking to the curriculum taught in another subject area; combining together two or more curricula; and drawing from disciplines outside of language arts—offer students a chance to make connections and applications beyond traditional ideas of English language arts.

We have found that developing and teaching integrated units supports our students to acquire the important thinking skills necessary to develop deep understandings. The development of thinking skills and conceptual understanding braid together well. At the same time, integrating units has helped us to figure out what are the key ideas of a unit (and discipline) and, as a result, we are better able to facilitate deep learning.

It's not just the ideas of a subject area or discipline that can be integrated. Leyton remembers visiting Joanne's classroom a few years back when several Grade 8 teachers were focusing on the thinking skill of making connections. Joanne was modeling how she made connections to her English 8 students. When she asked them to describe how they made connections, two boys explained how their science teacher had shown them how to make connections when looking at different systems in the body. During the boys' description, one girl exclaimed, "Oh, that's what he was trying to show us!" This student finally realized what one teacher was doing when she saw another teacher using the same strategy. Over the course of her unit, Joanne was able to build on her students' experience in science and help students develop this practice in English. Having opportunities to use and apply the same thinking skill within different content areas helps students become more successful thinkers and learners in both subject areas. What we've realized is that, in fact, these thinking skills help students understand concepts in content areas more deeply.

Cross-Curricular Planning and Teaching

Cross-curricular teaching and learning can help us "make the familiar strange." We're often so used to teaching what we teach in the way that we teach it that we don't see things from students' perspectives. Combining subject areas gives us a reason to think about what we are choosing to teach, why we are choosing to teach these particular concepts and thinking skills, and how we will teach them. We believe that we have a stronger impact on student learning when we develop and teach units that integrate big ideas from various subject areas, approaches that support diversity, and thinking skills and strategies.

We want learning to feel coherent for students. Integrated units tend to span longer periods of time as we deeply explore key ideas from multiple perspectives. For instance, Leyton worked with Linda Watson and Eve Minuk to develop a unit that studied the question *What makes Napoleon an enduring historical figure?* Through this unit they were able to address learning outcomes from language arts and social studies. Consciously planning to address and assess outcomes from two subject areas, they created text sets that included fiction and nonfiction, historical and present-day writing, and shorter and longer texts that all connected to the actions of individuals and their impact on their community and broader society.

We also find that we can better meet the diverse learning needs of our students within an integrated unit. Rather than having to keep track of multiple assignments in different subject areas, a cross-curricular unit can help students focus on fewer, more in-depth tasks. Within these units, students get multiple opportunities to investigate, discuss, read, and write about key ideas. Just as they would be engrossed in a novel, we want students engaging deeply with ideas, questions, and issues over time.

As we have discussed throughout this book, when we delve into a topic over time we need to use key skills and strategies that help us explore and acquire related enduring understandings. Thus, we develop and teach mini-lessons that help students more successfully learn and demonstrate their understanding. Approaching planning and teaching this way has moved us away from genre-based and isolated skill- or strategy-oriented teaching to developing targeted skills and strategies over the course of a unit. Perhaps more importantly, together as a class we can explicitly examine how certain skills are important for, and specific to, disciplinary study (history, the sciences, etc.). This gives students the opportunity to develop and use skills and strategies in ways that have more authentic real-world applications.

Where possible, we look for ways to integrate subject areas and to collaborate with other teachers. As we develop units and tasks that make connections between subject areas, we help students to see how ideas are woven together. Knowledge and skills in one discipline are useful in other areas of study.

Middle and elementary school teachers often teach the same group of students more than one subject. This offers a way to integrate two or more subjects. On page 136 you meet Nicole Widdess and Sue Gall, who typically alternate integrating science and social studies with English language arts in their Grade 6/7 classrooms.

- One practical way to organize an integrated unit is to teach humanities as an integrated subject area. Some schools in our school district offer Humanities 8 and/or 9 as a course. The Integrating Language Arts and Social Studies example in this chapter comes from when Alecia and Mehjabeen taught Humanities 8 and 9. This kind of course organization encourages teachers to create integrated units.
- In middle and secondary schools, subject-area teachers who teach their courses in the same time period can often collaborate to co-plan and co-teach. For example, Mehjabeen taught a Social Studies 8 class at the same time as a colleague who taught Science 8, so they were able to co-plan and co-teach an integrated science and social studies unit to their 60 students.
- A third way to link English language arts to another content area is to find out from colleagues what topics they will be covering in their courses. In British Columbia, students learn about Canada's role in WWII in Social

Studies 11. English teachers might teach a thematic unit in which they choose literature that explores this event.

Core Understandings: Integrating Content Areas

Integrated units...

- provide students with the time and place to explore ideas more deeply.
- encourage students to think about concepts from multiple perspectives.
- help students see connections across subject areas they might otherwise miss.
- provide opportunities for students to develop the thinking skills necessary to be able to connect across subject areas and disciplines.
- prepare students to participate in a world where they need to make connections across more specialized bodies of knowledge.
- can help us work more closely with our colleagues and encourage professional development.
- increase the relevance of class work for students. As soon as they see applicability of ideas beyond a single classroom, they see them as more relevant.
- may help capture student interests by bringing in areas or topics from other subject areas that students find engaging.

Examples from our Classrooms

We don't believe in teaching strategies for strategies' sake or content for content's sake. We want our students to be able to tackle real-world issues and tasks in real-world environments where they need to call upon the higher-level thinking skills and content. We live in a world where knowledge and information is expanding at an ever-increasing rate, and our task now is to teach students how to make sense of and use and apply this knowledge. The explicit teaching of thinking skills gives them access to content that is often compartmentalized and remote. Teaching at least some integrated units will help students be able to think in ways that will equip them for the 21st century.

Integrating Science and English Language Arts

In this learning sequence, Grade 6/7 teachers Sue Gall and Nicole Widdess planned collaboratively with Leyton to develop a unit focusing on science content while simultaneously targeting and building reading and thinking skills from English language arts. During their planning they found that they could easily help students meet learning outcomes from both the science and language arts curricula by engaging students with inquiry questions that required them to learn through reading, discussions, and hands-on field studies.

After taking time to reflect on the profile of Nicole and Sue's classes, the teachers set goals for student learning to be demonstrated by the end of their Ecosystems unit. They wanted students to be better at

- determining importance
- applying their learning across English and Science tasks (and beyond!)
- planning and self-monitoring their use of strategies

- using their thinking strategies and content knowledge when engaging in an authentic task
- transforming what they learned into a mini-documentary using their inquiry skills and technology

By working on these goals for students, they were able to address and assess multiple outcomes, some from the science curriculum, some from the ELA curriculum, and some that overlapped.

ENDURING UNDERSTANDINGS FOR UNIT

Looking at the ecology-related outcomes, Sue, Nicole, and Leyton found that they could focus student learning for the unit around three big ideas:

1. Human beings are keepers of an Earth in which everything is connected.
2. To survive, organisms depend on one another to break down, recycle, and transfer food/energy/chemicals.
3. Our actions can sustain or damage an ecosystem.

ESSENTIAL QUESTIONS

One of the things Sue, Leyton, and Nicole love about cross-curricular planning and teaching is delving deeply into both the topic and the related thinking strategies and processes. This allows them to develop a multi-week unit incorporating inquiry and reading/thinking strategies. To engage students and focus their learning, they developed weekly inquiry questions that related back to the unit's big idea. These questions helped focus their teaching and students' learning for the week.

Nicole, Sue, and Leyton see learning in science and language arts as a process of constructing meaning and increasingly complex understandings about how the world and its systems work. Rather than telling students a big idea for the unit, Sue and Nicole pose it as a question to be investigated, inviting students into the process of constructing meaning. To explore the big ideas they identified for the unit, Nicole, Sue, and Leyton developed three inquiry questions that were central to the unit:

- How can we honor the interconnectedness of our environment?
- How are humans affecting the environment?
- What can we do to sustain the environment?

STRATEGY FOCUS

With the big idea, their class profiles, and the goals for their students in mind, they committed to developing a unit that included

- a connecting, processing, and transforming/personalizing lesson structure
- multimodal representation opportunities (differentiation)
- opportunities for students to plan and reflect on learning activities

They organized the unit so that students developed their understanding of important science concepts using fiction and nonfiction texts while at the same time developing the key thinking strategies they had identified.

ASSESSMENT

Leyton, Nicole, and Sue find that students immerse themselves in a unit of study when they are working with key questions and an end task in mind. Based on the inquiry questions, they brainstormed what the final summative assessment would look like.

END-OF-UNIT ASSESSMENT

Ecosystems: Performance Assessment

Using your skills and knowledge from this unit, create a mini-documentary with a partner or on your own. Use iMovie and GarageBand to show your thinking.

Your mini-documentary should focus on one of the following questions:
• How are humans affecting the environment?
• What can we do to help sustain the environment?

Planning
a. Begin by researching your topic using what we've learned to date and information from other resources such as books, magazines, newspapers, the Internet, and interviews.
b. Re-watch the YouTube vignettes that we looked at together. As you watch, think about what actions are affecting the environment positively or negatively. Be prepared to discuss your observations.
c. Using the information you have gathered, develop a storyboard that sketches out your mini-documentary. Include simple images and incorporate words or sentences you may wish to record.

Please hand in your planning pages.

Mini-Documentary: Your project should be informative and answer one of the two questions above. The documentary should be 1.5 to 2 minutes long.

Celebrate: Share your mini-documentary with the class.

Lesson Sequence

A learning sequence often takes more than one class to complete the phases of connect, process, transform/personalize.

To develop the knowledge and skills students needed to complete the summative assessment, Sue, Nicole, and Leyton planned a set of lesson sequences. These sequences were organized around weekly inquiry questions.

Week	1	2	3	4
Inquiry Questions	What does it mean to pay attention to or learn from the environment?	What do organisms need to survive?	What is an ecosystem?	What living and non-living things make up an ecosystem?
Key Ideas/ Information (Know)	• We learn through observation. • We can learn by noticing connections and relationships in nature's systems and cultures. • We need to pay attention to and be responsible for the impact of our actions.	• Organisms need light, air, water to survive.	• An environment shared by organisms with particular characteristics • Set of relationships and interactions	• Soil • Water • Air • Sunlight

Week	5	6
Inquiry Questions	What can we learn by exploring our own ecosystems?	How do living things share or interact in an ecosystem?
Lesson Topic (Know)	• Conduct an Investigation • School Habitat • Minoru Park	• Producers, consumers • Food web/chain • Energy and chemical transfer

Week	7	8	9
Inquiry Questions	How are food webs important to ecosystems?	How are humans affecting the environment? (case studies and field studies)	
Lesson Topic (Know)	Food Web		

Week	10	11	12
Inquiry Questions	How are we affecting the environment? What can we do to sustain the environment?	Creating mini-documentaries	
Lesson Topic (Know)	All concepts taught to date from the ecosystems unit	Mini-lessons revisiting key ideas, thinking skills, and technology as needed	

Lesson 1: What Does It Mean to Pay Attention to/Learn from the Environment?

Rather than use the term "ecosystem," we began with a more familiar term—"the environment."

1. Connect: Begin by asking the class what it means to pay attention to or learn from the environment.
   • Students work in groups of three to ask the same question, much like an interview, and record their partners' thinking on the front of the Lesson 1 Organizer. We hope that students will come up with answers that include the ideas of observing, analyzing, interpreting.
   • Provide enough time for students to explore their thinking; then ask three or four students to share what they learned from their partners. At this point, let students know that they might hear an idea that they didn't think of and it is okay to add it to their organizer.
   • If students do not come up with answers that include the words *observe, analyze, interpret*, offer these terms to the class for consideration.

LESSON 1 ORGANIZER: FRONT

What does it mean to pay attention to or learn from the environment?

Connect	Using the question above, interview two partners. Record their response below: Partner 1: Partner 2:
Process	Listen to the picture book *Just a Dream*, by Chris Van Allsburg, and fill in the four quadrants on the back of this page.
Transform/ Personalize	Thinking back to the story…. How did one or more of the characters pay attention and make a difference?

LESSON 1 ORGANIZER: BACK

Observe…	Wonder…
Feel…	Actions taken…

Adapted from Brownlie and Close (1992)

2. Process: With the previous question in mind, have students complete a Four Quadrants on the back of the Lesson 1 Organizer as you read Chris Van Allsburg's picture book, *Just a Dream*.
   • We chose this picture book because it was a good way to build background knowledge about humans' relationship to the environment. We want students to listen and jot down what the main character observes, wonders, and feels, and what actions the character takes.
   • Begin by modeling how to complete the quadrants as you read. It is most effective if you can model this strategy with two teachers, both thinking aloud about what they are drawing from the story and jotting down their ideas on a copy of the graphic organizer. We usually put a copy of the graphic organizer on the overhead projector so that students can see us jotting down ideas.
   • As we continue to read the book, students elicit ideas and jot them down on their graphic organizers. Stop every few pages and ask students to share their thinking with a partner and/or have students come up to the overhead to record their thinking.
3. Transform/Personalize: Looking at the ideas they collected in their four quadrants, ask students to think more deeply about the actions that the character took in the book to help his environment.
   • Model what this might look like for you.
   • Ask students to talk about this with their table groups and to record their thinking on the organizer.

Lesson 2: How Can We Pay Attention to Ecosystems?

1. Connect: This phase of the lesson helps students think about ideas they encountered the day before and access their prior knowledge about the role of observation.
   - Encourage students to talk with their partners around the *What?*, *So What?*, and *Now What?* of taking action based on observations.
   - Provide enough time for a thoughtful conversation so that students feel successful in getting some ideas down.
   - Stop after each question and record class ideas.
2. Process: Students use magnet notes to record their thinking.
   - They read a chunk (usually one or two paragraphs) of a text describing ecosystems and how they work; they identify the most important word. This becomes the magnet word and is recorded in the centre of the sticky note.
   - Students reread the chunk and look for no more than four or five words that attract to the magnet word. These are recorded around the magnet word.
   - Finally, using the words on the magnet note, students develop a sentence summary using at least four of the words.
3. Transform/Personalize: At this point, students will have read about ecosystems, so it's time to start using the term.
   - Ask students to record how we can pay attention to what goes on in ecosystems. You can offer students a choice of how to represent this information.
   - If we want to give students personalized feedback on their note-making, we assess student thinking for chunk 4, as it is done independently.
   - We also offer descriptive feedback about the logic of their thinking related to our synthesis question: *How we can pay attention to what goes on in an ecosystem?*

The use of magnet notes is adapted from Buehl (2001). We suggest using gradual release to teach this strategy. The teacher reads the first chunk of the text and creates a magnet note. Students can copy or adapt what has been modeled for chunk 1. Students then complete chunks 2 and 3 with a partner, and chunk 4 independently.

LESSON 2 ORGANIZER

Connect	**What?**
	What techniques are important when paying attention?
	So What?
	Why are they important?
	Now What?
	What actions can we take?

Process	What do organisms need to survive? Show your understanding by using magnet notes while reading the text.
	Chunk 1 [Sticky notes] Paragraph Summary:
	Chunk 2 [Sticky notes] Paragraph Summary:
	Chunk 3 [Sticky notes] Paragraph Summary:
	Chunk 4 [Sticky notes] Paragraph Summary:
Transform/Personalize	**How can we pay attention to what goes on in ecosystems?** Show your thinking through words, images, and diagrams.

Lesson 3: What Is an Ecosystem?

1. Connect: Again, in the connecting phase of the lesson, help students review the previous lesson.
   - Students can refer to their previous organizer to complete the *Connect* part of the organizer independently.
   - Students share their thoughts aloud to the whole class once they have had a chance to jot down some ideas. (We call this "thinking time.")
2. Process: Ask students to work in partners to look at diagrams of ecosystems you have collected from the Internet or sourced from a textbook.
   - Students choose one diagram that they would like to focus on.
   - Ask students to describe what they see and how they think aspects of the diagram are related.
   - For some students this can be challenging; if so, take time to model this with the class. With one class we had students work in table groups and represent their thoughts on chart paper to share with the whole class, in an effort to help students analyze how aspects of an ecosystem are related.
3. Transform/Personalize: We keep asking the students to think about what it is they need in order to pay attention to something, such as the environment or organisms. We do this to help students synthesize what they are learning while also building their observational and analytical think skills.
   - Have students show their emerging understandings of ecosystems, using the information they learned from analyzing the diagrams, by recording their thinking in a thought bubble and adding words and images.
   - Ask students to highlight three words or images in their thought bubble that they are most proud of and want you to focus on when assessing their work.

LESSON 3 ORGANIZER

Connect	Use pictures, words or diagrams to **show what an organism needs to survive.**
Process	**Examine one of the diagrams to help propose principles of an ecosystem.** Think/Pair/Share: What do you see? How are things related?
Transform/ Personalize	**What do we need to pay attention to when studying an ecosystem?** Show your thinking in a thought bubble.

Lesson 4: What Living and Non-Living Things Make up an Ecosystem?

1. Connect: With students in groups of four, provide a placemat (Bennett & Rolheiser, 2001) to each group; see template on page 153.
   - Ask students to complete what they think the quotes on the Lesson 4 Graphic Organizer mean to them.
   - In a placemat, students get a box to brainstorm what they know and believe about a quote, question, or statement. Then each student shares what they have recorded.
   - After sharing, ask groups to record what they think are the most likely meanings of the quote. Have them write this in the centre circle of their chart.
   - Ask one member of each group to share their two ideas out.
   - Groups can add ideas they hear from others on their placemats.
2. Process: Using a Venn diagram, ask students to read the section in their textbooks (or an article, podcast, or other form of text) that focuses on the differences and similarities of living and non-living things.
   - Model what this looks like to students using the first chunk (paragraph) of the text.
   - Assess student Venn diagrams based on accuracy of content.
3. Transform/Personalize: By this point we feel like we need some feedback from students on how things are going, not just for this particular lesson, but also for the unit to date.
   - We ask students to complete an exit slip that we read and use for future lesson planning. We provide sentence starters; however, we also encourage students to respond in a way that worked best for them.

See page 153 for Placemat Template.

Connect	**Look at the following quotes. Reflect on what you think these quotes mean and why they are important.** "As a people we have developed a life-style that is draining the earth of its priceless and irreplaceable resources without regard for the future of our children and people all around the world." (Margaret Mead) "The earth does not belong to man; man belongs to the earth. This we know. All things are connected like the blood which unites a family. All things are connected." (Chief Seattle)
Process	**What do living and non-living things have in common? What's different?** Using the information from the text, work together to complete the Venn diagram on the back of this page.
Transform/ Personalize	**Exit Slip** Respond to one of the following sentence starters or create your own. • I learned… • The key ideas are… • Question(s) I have include…

Unit Reflection

- Sue, Leyton, and Nicole are finding that their students are more engaged in their Ecosystems unit, now that they use guiding questions and require students to find information, reflect on it, and collaboratively construct their understandings of a concept.
- They find that their gradual release of the development of thinking skills such as observation, determining importance, note-making, and synthesis helps their students focus on and develop enduring understandings.
- Using fiction and nonfiction to develop analysis and thinking skills addresses learning outcomes from both English language arts and science. Integrating these two subject areas has given them more time to delve deeply into important questions related to ecosystems.
- Perhaps most importantly, they find that creating a summative assessment that links the overarching big ideas of the unit—the interconnectedness of the environment and the ways that humans affect ecosystems—offers students opportunities to personalize, apply, and transform what they learn. As they move through the unit Sue and Nicole are able to develop students' capacity to represent and thus communicate their understandings through storyboards and multimedia technology.

It is interesting to note that Alecia, Julie Anne, and Erin taught this unit in a French Immersion setting, integrating French language arts and social studies curricula.

Integrating Language Arts and Social Studies

This unit on Ancient China was taught in Humanities 8 by Mehjabeen, Baren Tsui, and Alecia Payne, and was originally co-planned by Mehjabeen, Krista,

Julie Anne Mainville, Erin Steele, and Catriona Misfeldt. Humanities is a course that combines language arts and social studies.

This unit was taught a couple of months into the school year and built on the visualization strategies that were taught at the beginning of the year using fiction. It is a good example of how the thinking strategies of visualization and determining importance taught in language arts can become ways of developing understanding of social studies content.

In the months preceding the teaching of this unit, students were taught how to use visualization as a way to express and summarize their thinking as they read novels in literature circles. They would record the images that came into their minds as they were reading, and eventually started to summarize their thinking in images. By drawing or writing down images as they read, students were able to interact with and make meaning from the texts they were reading, as well as to hold on to the thinking they experienced as they read. As they were recording images, they were also writing notes on the main characters in their novels. Once they finished their novels, they created a mind map on their character, using both images and the notes on character.

Both the visualization and the mind-mapping became key strategies used in the unit on Ancient China. In this unit, teachers could now use this visualization strategy to have students work with myth and nonfiction texts. Students also work on determining importance and note-making using a variety of strategies, including the mind-mapping strategy.

ENDURING UNDERSTANDINGS FOR UNIT

1. There are a number of factors that influence the development and decline of civilizations.
2. Geographical features and climate affect the world view and the development of civilizations.
3. The world views held by people of Ancient China were derived from their beliefs and influenced the development of their civilization.
4. Arts, culture, science, technology, and education evolve and are refined as societies develop and interact.

UNIT OBJECTIVES

• Students will develop an understanding of the society and perspectives of the people of the Ancient China and how these were derived from geography, myth, and systems of belief.
• Students will understand how one society builds on and incorporates the beliefs and systems of the one before it.
• Students will develop the reading skills of visualization and determining importance in fiction and nonfiction. They will also develop note-taking skills using a variety of strategies.
• Students will learn how to write paragraphs.

ASSESSMENT

• Formative Assessment: visualization activities; mind maps and note-making tables; paragraphs
• Summative Assessment: at least one paragraph; Shang and Zhou Dynasties test; Shang-to-Tang composition or visual

Lesson 1: Components of Civilization

1. Students are asked two questions: *What is civilization, and what are the components of civilization?*
   • As a class, students brainstorm the major components of civilization.
   • Building on the class brainstorm and discussion, teachers rephrase the enduring understandings for the unit so that they reflect the students' ideas:

   1. Geography affects the development of a civilization.
   2. Civilization is made up of beliefs, art, people, technology, and science, and these things evolve as society develops.

   • By the end of the unit, these understandings will be refined further and then carried into the study of other civilizations. The two above are from one of Mehjabeen's classes.
2. The class creates a general mind map template organizing the various components of civilization. This mind map is posted on the wall for students to refer to throughout the year.

Lesson 2: Geography and Civilization

1. Students first complete a map of the geography of China in order to understand where Ancient China was located and what geographical features were in its proximity.
   • They look at each geographical feature separately to think about its impact.
   • As a class they discuss the ways that each geographical feature affects civilization. Students' ideas are recorded below.

SAMPLE TABLE FOR CHINA: GEOGRAPHY AND CIVILIZATION

Geographical Feature of China	How this feature affects civilization
Rivers	• Provide fresh water for drinking, provide food (fish), make nearby land fertile – therefore people like to live near water and build cities • Transportation – people can travel to other places – allows for exchange of goods and ideas
Mountains	Difficult to cross - create barriers between people
Deserts	Difficult to cross – create barriers between people
Plateaus	Can sometimes provide good farmland, other times becomes a barrier
Oceans	Can provide access to other places but are also divides as they are so large

2. Students look at all of the factors together to think about what overall effects the geography of China would have had on its people.
   • By looking at each factor separately and then together, students were able to infer two of the main ideas of the unit: that people tend to build communities around rivers; and that the geography of China forced its people

This sequence is adapted from Wilhelm (2004).

to remain isolated from other societies as there were many natural barriers.

3. In order to develop the skill of inference, students are led through a visualization sequence.
   • In this sequence, we have students infer a main idea by asking them to look at a group of objects/points/images and to guess what the main idea is.
   • We start with a small group of objects/points/images and ask students to guess. We slowly add objects/points/images until students have narrowed down the main idea to what we want them to infer.
   • We first model this sequence using the names of the students in the class (main idea = students in the class).
   • We then model it using the geographic features of the city of Richmond (main idea = geography of Richmond) where we teach.
   • The third time we lead the students through the sequence, we use the geographic features of China (main idea = the geography of China both isolates and protects it).

Lesson 3: The Creation Myth of Pangu

1. Next students read the creation myth "Pangu" aloud with the teacher.
   • This myth connects to the beliefs of Ancient China that students are about to learn and also to the geography that they have just learned.
   • As they read the myth, students use visualization as a note-taking strategy, recording in the margins the images they see as they read the text.
   • Students have been using this visualization strategy when reading their novels. However, in order to ensure that they transfer this strategy effectively to the reading of myth and later nonfiction, the teachers model this visualization on a whiteboard or overhead transparency.
2. After completing the reading, students pull out the main ideas of the myth.
   • By looking at their images, students can see that the most dominant images they have recorded are those of the creation of heaven and earth and of the development of China's geographical features.

Lesson 4: The Great Wall

1. Students are given a short text about the Great Wall and a list of vocabulary from the text.
   • We go over with the students, as a group, different strategies they have learned already for finding meaning in unknown words.
   • After doing some examples with the students, we ask them to read the text and make predictions of what the new vocabulary words mean.
   • When they finish, students are asked to verify their predictions in a dictionary and write the correct definition on their sheet if necessary.
2. After completing the vocabulary exercise, students are given a list of questions and asked to answer by stating what they think is important and what they think is interesting.
   • The addition of the second element of the question makes students feel that their interests are valued, and this deepens their engagement with the text. They are happy to share their answers when the class debriefs.

- As students go through this exercise, they see how the ideas they are thinking about connect to the geography of China and the perspectives and beliefs of its peoples.

Lesson 5: Belief Systems

1. There were three main beliefs held by the people of Ancient China: the belief in Dualism or the Yin/Yang; belief in Ancestor Worship; and belief in the Mandate of Heaven.
   - These three beliefs are very difficult for students to grasp. In order to ensure that students develop deep understandings of these beliefs, we use the strategies of visualization and paraphrasing.
   - We provide students with notes on these beliefs and, as they talk about each belief, students have to paraphrase and then summarize each of the beliefs.
2. After working through the notes, students are asked to create a visual that shows how each of these three beliefs were perceived by the people of Ancient China.
3. We model the writing of a paragraph using these three beliefs as the content.
   - As the unit continues, students use this initial model of paragraph writing as a reference for further paragraph writing.

Lesson 6: Note-Making and the Shang Dynasty

1. We chose two-column notes as the note-taking strategy to be used for this unit.
   - The two columns are entitled *What's Important* and *Why?*
   - Students are asked to pull out important details from the textbook and to use the enduring understandings from the unit as a reference. What this means is that whatever fact they write down from the text, they have to explain how it contributed to the development of Chinese civilization.
   - Teachers model on an overhead transparency, using a think-aloud, how to pull out information and how to connect it to the enduring understandings.
   - The class then begins taking notes together.
2. When the note-taking is finished, students are given a mind-map template, based on the one that was originally created, to help them organize their information.
   - The mind map is completed as a class.
   - To complete the mind map, students draw on the information from their note-taking as well as the notes they received about beliefs.
   - The mind map helps students organize the information from their notes under main idea headings.

Lesson 7: Continuing Note-Making and the Zhou Dynasty

1. Students attempt two-column notes independently for the Zhou Dynasty; they complete the same mind-map template for the Zhou dynasty.
   - As they take these notes, students observe that changes occurred in the beliefs (Mandate of Heaven) and make the connection between the fall of the Shang and the rise of the Zhou.

2. Using the model of the paragraph on the beliefs of Ancient China, students write a paragraph on one aspect of the Zhou Dynasty.
   - Teachers formatively assess these paragraphs and students set goals to either rewrite this paragraph or to improve their next one.
   - Teachers provide feedback by assessing on a rubric and identifying the following:

   1. What is working (what he/she did well)
   2. What is not working (what needs to be improved) and how it can be improved

   Student goal for next paragraph:_____

Lesson 8: Belief Systems and Comparison

1. Students are given a short text about Confucianism and asked to use their note-making strategy of *What's Important* and *Why?*
   - Using their notes, together as a class, students organize information under the main ideas of Beliefs, Values, and Actions; these are recorded in the *What's Important* column.
   - Students discuss how these were connected within the context of Confucianism, and how they influenced people's thinking and values; these are recorded in the *Why?* column.
   - As an enrichment activity, students analyze examples of Confucius' teachings and connect those examples back to the values of Confucianism.
2. Students repeat this process with a text on Taoism.
3. Students are given a Venn diagram template, and we model how to use the diagram to compare and contrast the two belief systems.
   - Students complete the diagram in small groups and then write paragraphs comparing the two beliefs. Again, these paragraphs are formatively assessed; students set goals and rewrite them; and then students submit final paragraphs to be graded summatively.

Lesson 9: Summative Assessment

At this point, students are about halfway through the unit. In order to summatively assess their learning to date and to provide them with a synthesis activity, we give them a short test on the material. It requires them to represent their knowledge of Chinese geography and history, using the same strategies that they have used for learning about them: visualization, note-making, and paragraph writing.

- Before giving them the test, we take them through a process of summarizing their notes and using visualization to remember key information. The purpose of this is to teach students how to prepare for a test. This "studying" process is also modeled and supported by teachers so that students are able to break down the thinking steps needed in remembering important information for a test.

- Below are some of the questions from the test that we used:

  - In the question on the creative myth of ancient China, students are provided with the option of showing their understanding in images or in a written summary.
  - When asked to share their knowledge of the different components of Chinese civilization, students have to place the information they know into a table, and then synthesize and connect it in a Venn diagram. The graphic organizers are ones that they are already familiar with and support them in thinking about what information to write down and why.
  - For the final part of the test, students have to write a paragraph on one of the concepts that they have learned about during the unit thusfar. The paragraph is assessed with the same criteria and rubric that is used throughout the unit for formative and summative assessment.

Lessons 9–15: *Medieval Chian (Qin–Tang)*

- Following the test, we teach students how to build on their notes from the Shang and Zhou dynasties to access information and learn about the development of China during the medieval period.
- Using the format of a large chart or table, students take notes on the next few dynasties, focusing on how each one *developed* from the other (this is one of the enduring understandings from the unit).
- We model the taking of notes again with the Qin dynasty; we teach students how to infer main ideas about the development of Chinese religion and government from looking both across the rows and down the columns of the table.

See sample table below; changes highlighted in **bold.**

1. Fill in information from the Shang and Zhou Dynasties (students already know this) and highlight the changes (development).
2. Model note-taking on Qin Dynasty and highlight the changes since Zhou Dynasty.
3. Model note-taking on Han, Sui, and Tang Dynasties and highlight the changes to show the development of Chinese religion and government over time.

Component of Civilization	Shang	Zhou	Qin	Han	Sui	Tang
Religion	• Shang-ti • Many gods • Ancestor worship	• Tien • Many gods • Ancestor worship • **Mandate of Heaven** • **Taoism** • **Confucianism** • **Legalism**	• Tien • Many gods • Ancestor worship • Mandate of Heaven • Taoism • Confucianism • Legalism	• Tien • Many gods • Ancestor worship • Mandate of Heaven • Taoism • Confucianism • Legalism • **Buddhism (last three most common)**	• Tien • Many gods • Ancestor worship • Mandate of Heaven • Taoism • Confucianism • Legalism • **Buddhism – most common** •	• Tien • Many gods • Ancestor worship • Mandate of Heaven • Taoism • Confucianism • Legalism • Buddhism

Component of Civilization	Shang	Zhou	Qin	Han	Sui	Tang
						• Silk Road – leads to introduction of religions of India and Middle East (Judaism, Christianity, Islam)
Government	Feudal land divided into regions and ruled by nobles	Feudal land divided into regions and ruled by nobles	Land divided in to regions and **ruled by officials appointed by emperor Legalism**	**Become an official based on "MERIT" by writing exams**	**Continued exam system of Han**	

4. Students takes notes on the other components of civilization (e.g., arts, culture, technology, people, etc.) in the same table and track their development in a similar way.

Lesson 16: Mind Map on the Silk Road

The final dynasty students learn about is the Tang Dynasty, which is influenced by the Silk Toad and the interchange of culture and peoples that occurs as a result. Students create large group mind maps on the different ideas and goods introduced into China from the Silk Road and how they affected civilization there.

Lesson 17: Shang–Tang: Final Synthesis and Summative Assessment

1. The final assignment for the unit on China requires students to explain how Chinese civilization developed from the Shang to the Tang Dynasties in three areas (choose from religion, government, people, technology, arts, culture, etc.).
   • Students usually write a composition or create a large visual showing their understanding of this development.
   • We model how to write a composition and use transitions to make connections and comparisons across the dynasties; we model writing introductions and conclusions.
   • For this assignment, students are primarily assessed on their knowledge and understanding, and for the coherence of each of their paragraphs. Later in the year, we do another development composition assignment where students are assessed for writing skills such as transitions, introductions, and conclusions.

Unit Reflection

- This is a long unit that can take up to two and a half months of the year. For us, it has been time worth spending, as students develop many foundational skills for working with content areas.
- What is key for us is the focus on the thinking skills of visualization, inference, determining importance, and summarizing that allow students to deeply understand the complex ideas and information that they are being taught. What is exciting for us is to hear and read students' understanding of a culture and civilization very distant to them across time and space.
- By spending this extended time developing thinking skills, we have found that our students are able to grasp increasingly complex ideas and synthesize information and concepts with insight and appreciation. We continue to have students use these thinking skills to learn about other civilizations for the remainder of the year.
- The outcome that provides us with the most satisfaction as teachers is that, by taking our students deeply into the understanding of cultures and civilizations, we help them to develop the ability and sensitivity to appreciate diversity and difference.

Placemat Template

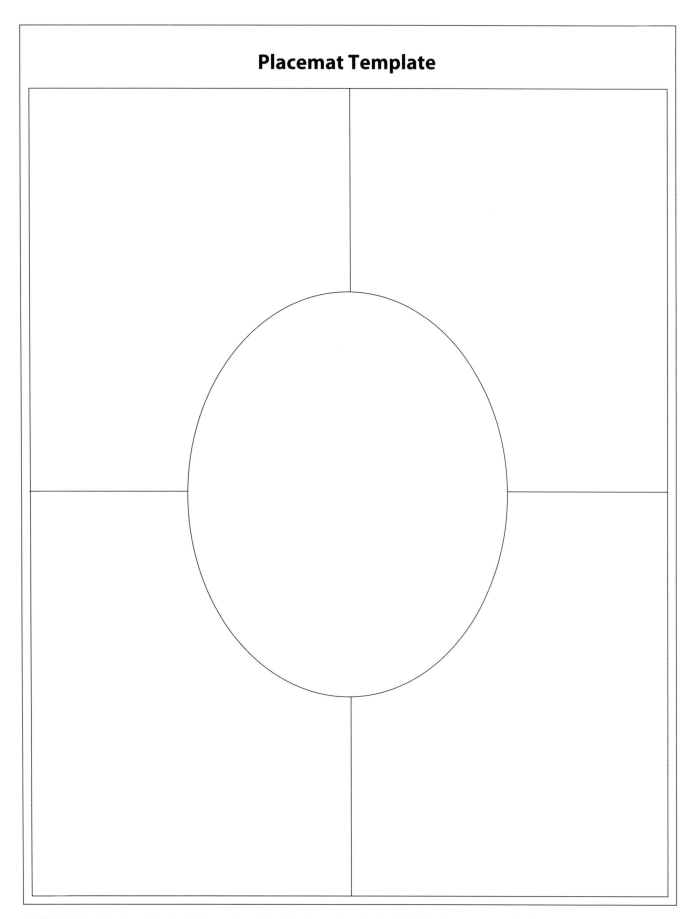

Conclusion: Looking Back, Thinking Ahead

• What can we do as teachers to further encourage student engagement?
• What can we do, personally and structurally, to create more time and opportunity to collaborate?
• How can we continue to be engaged as teachers and learners in our profession?

The work we do together helps make things clearer to us so that, when we explain a unit to students, we're much more coherent about our purpose, intention, processes. When we know why we're doing what we're doing, it's a lot easier to be responsive and negotiate learning with students. Now, when our students challenge us, we include their concerns in our own questioning.

Teaching is alive for us. Even as we write this conclusion, we are thinking about ideas for different units and ways we can improve units. We are never finished with our inquiry and growth as teachers and learners. We started our collaboration looking for answers, but in a way we just found better questions…

Ownership and engagement are as important for us as they are for our students. Working together is invigorating. Part of what makes it so is that we are constantly trying new things. We support each other through the messy process of trying things out, making mistakes and learning from them.

When we ask ourselves what keeps us so interested in teaching, we recognize the importance of the process of collaboration and inquiry: having conversations, building units together, working through practices, exploring new ideas, pushing each other outside our comfort zones, questioning each other. We continue to widen our circle of questioning and inquiry from our own classrooms to spaces within our schools and other learning communities. In a way, it has become our way of being. The more we value collaboration, the more we engage and find joy in teaching.

Being connected with each other supports us to extend our care to others, particularly our students and colleagues. Talking with our colleagues about what is working or not working in our classrooms, seeking out opportunities to plan a lesson sequence, and joining study groups to explore current educational thinking, adolescent literature book clubs, and writing groups—these are all ways that we can connect with other teachers. These learning communities nurture and sustain us, and are at the heart of our professional development.

We have several new questions to explore:

• How can we prepare our students for a world that we cannot yet imagine?
• How is learning and teaching transforming as a result of new literacies?
• How do the structures of school, including curriculum design, need to change to reflect the changes in the world around us?

We look forward to the messiness and excitement that exploring these questions together will bring.

Bibliography/Professional Resources

Albright, J. (2000) "Oracy, critical theory and secondary English education: travelling towards a reconceptualized discipline." In B. Barrell & R. Hammett (Eds.), *Advocating change: Contemporary issues in subject English.* (215–226). Toronto, ON: Irwin Publishing.

Alvermann, D.E. (2002) "Effective literacy instruction for adolescents." *Journal of Literacy Research, 34*(2), 189–208.

Atwell, N. (1998) *In the middle: New understandings about writing, reading, and learning.* Portsmouth, NH: Heinemann.

Atwell, N. (2007) *The reading zone: How to help kids become skilled, passionate, habitual, critical readers.* New York, NY: Scholastic.

Beers, K. (2003) *When kids can't read – what teachers can do: A guide for teachers 6–12.* Portsmouth, NH: Heinemann.

Belanger, J., Allingham, P.V. & Béchervaise, N. (2005) "'When will we ever learn?': The case for formative assessment supporting writing development." *English in Australia, 141,* 41–48.

Bennett, B. & Rolheiser, C. (2001) *Beyond Monet: The artful science of instructional integration.* Toronto, ON: Bookation Inc.

Bransford, J., Brown, A. & Cocking, R. (Eds.) (2000) *How people learn: Brain, mind, experience, and school.* Washington, DC: National Academies Press.

Brownlie, F. (2009) "Adolescent Literacy Assessment: Finding Out What You Need to Know." In S.R. Parris, D. Fisher, & K. Headley (Eds.) *Adolescent Literacy, Field Tested* (117–125). Newark, DE: International Reading Association.

Brownlie, F. (2005) *Grand conversations, thoughtful responses: A unique approach to literature circles.* Winnipeg, MB: Portage and Main Press.

Brownlie, F. & Close, S. (1992) *Beyond Chalk and Talk.* Markham, ON: Pembroke

Brownlie, F. & Feniak, C. (1998) *Student diversity.* Markham, ON: Pembroke.

Brownlie, F., Feniak, C. & Schnellert, L. (2006) *Student diversity: Classroom strategies to meet the learning needs of all students* (2nd ed.). Markham, ON: Pembroke.

Brownlie, F. & King, J. (2000) *Learning in safe schools: creating classrooms where all students belong.* Markham, ON: Pembroke.

Brownlie, F. &. Schnellert, L. (2009) *All about thinking: Collaborating to support all learners.* Winnipeg, MB: Portage & Main Press.

Buehl, D. (2001) *Classroom strategies for interactive learning* (2nd ed.). Newark, DE: International Reading Association.

Bullock, J. (1998) *Why workshop? Changing course in 7–12 English.* Portland, ME: Stenhouse.

Burke, J. (2001) *Illuminating texts: How to teach students to read the world.* Portsmouth, NH: Heinemann.

Butler, D. L. & Schnellert, L. (2008) "Teachers working to achieve valued outcomes for students: Making meaningful links between research and practice." *Education Canada 48* (5) 36–40.

Butler, D.L., Schnellert, L. & Cartier, S.C. (2005) "Adolescents' engagement in "reading to learn": Bridging from assessment to instruction." *BC Educational Leadership Research, 2,* Retrieved December 12, 2008, from http://slc.educ.ubc.ca/ eJournal/index.htm.

Canadian Broadcasting Corporation (CBC) *The Age of Persuasion.* Episode, "The YouTube Revolution," http://www.cbc.ca/ageofpersuasion/2008/09/ the_youtube_revolution.html

Daniels, H. & Bizar, M. (2005) *Teaching the best practice way: Methods that matter, K–12.* Portland, ME: Stenhouse Publishers.

Fisher, D. & Frey, N. (2004) *Improving adolescent literacy.* Upper Saddle River, NJ: Pearson Merrill Prentice Hall.

Graham, P. "The Age of the Essay" (www.paulgraham .com/essay.html)

Graham, S. & Perin, D. (2007) *Writing next: Effective strategies to improve writing of adolescents in middle and high schools – A report to Carnegie Corporation of New York.* Washington, DC: Alliance for Excellent Education.

Gregory, K., Cameron, C. & Davies, A. (1997) *Setting and using criteria.* Courtenay, BC: Connections Publishing.

Gregory, K., Cameron, C. & Davies, A. (2000) *Self-assessment and goal setting: For use in middle and secondary school classrooms.* Courtenay, BC: Connections Publishing.

Guthrie, J.T. & Wigfield, A. (2000) "Engagement and motivation in reading." In M. L. Kamil, P.B.

Mosenthal, P.D. Pearson & R. Barr (Eds.) *Handbook of reading research.* (Vol. 3, 403–422). Mahwah, NJ: Erlbaum.

Harvey, S. & Goudvis, A. (2000) *Strategies that work: Teaching comprehension to enhance understanding.* Portland, ME: Stenhouse.

Ivey, G. & Fisher, D. (2006) *Creating literacy-rich schools for adolescents.* Alexandria, VA: ASCD.

Jones, P. (1988) *Lipservice: The story of talk in schools.* Philadelphia, PA: Open University Press.

Leggo, C. (1997) *Teaching to wonder: Responding to poetry in the secondary classroom.* Vancouver, BC: Pacific Education Press.

McClay, J. (2002) "Hidden 'treasure': New genres, new media, and the teaching of writing." *English in Education, 36*(1), 43–52.

Ministry of Education, Province of British Columbia (2006) *English language arts K to 7: Integrated Resource Package.* Online at http://www.bced.gov.bc.ca/ irp/irp_ela.htm

Ministry of Education, Province of British Columbia (2007) *English language arts 8 to 12: Integrated Resource Package.* Online at http://www.bced.gov. bc.ca/irp/irp_ela.htm

Ministry of Education, Province of British Columbia (2000) *Performance Standards for Reading and Writing.* Online at http://www.bced.gov.bc.ca/perf_ stands/

Moje, E.B., Young, J.P., Readence, J.E. & Moore, D.W. (2000) "Reinventing adolescent literacy for new times: Perennial and millennial issues." *Journal of Adolescent & Adult Literacy, 43,* 400–410.

National Writing Project & Nagin, C. (2003) *Because writing matters: Improving student writing in our schools.* San Francisco, CA: Josey-Bass.

New London Group (1996) "A pedagogy of multiliteracies: Designing social futures." *Harvard Educational Review, 66,* 60–92.

New London Group (2000) "A Pedagogy of Multiliteracies: Designing Social Futures." In Cope and Kalantzis (eds.) *Multiliteracies.* (9–37). London, UK: Routledge.

Palmer, Parker J. (1998) *The courage to teach: exploring the inner landscape of a teacher's life.* san Francisco, CA: Josey-Bass.

Pearson, P.D. & Gallagher, M.C. (1983) "The instruction of reading comprehension." *Contemporary Educational Psychology, 8*(3), 317–344.

Pressley, M. (2002) "Metacognition and self- regulated comprehension." In A. Farstrup & J. Samuels (eds.), *What research has to say about reading instruction* (291–309). Newark, DE: International Reading Association.

Probst, R. (2004) *Response and analysis: Teaching literature in secondary school* (2nd ed.). Portsmouth, NH: Heinemann.

Rief, L. (2006) "What's right with writing." *Voices from the Middle,* 13(4), 32–39.

Rosenblatt, L. (1994) *The reader, the text, the poem: The transactional theory of the literary work.* Carbondale, IL: Southern Illinois University Press.

Schnellert, L., Butler. D. & Higginson, S. (2008) "Co-constructors of data; co-constructors of meaning: Teacher professional development in an age of accountability." *Teaching and Teacher Education 24* (3) 725–750.

Shor, I. (1996) *When students have power: Negotiating authority in a critical pedagogy.* Chicago, IL: University of Chicago Press.

Siegel, M. (2006) "Rereading the sign: Multimodal transformations in the field of literacy education." In *Language Arts, 84,* 65–75.

Smith, M. & Wilhelm, J. (2006) *Going with the flow: How to engage boys (and girls) in their literacy learning.* Portsmouth, NH: Heinemann.

Steineke, N. (2002) *Reading and writing together: Collaborative literacy instruction in action.* New York, NY: Heinemann.

Tovani, C. (2000) *I read it, but I don't get it: Comprehension strategies for adolescent readers.* Portland, ME: Stenhouse.

Vinz, R. (2000) *Becoming other(wise): Enhancing critical reading perspectives.* Portland, ME: Calendar Island Publishers.

Vygotsky, L.S. (1978) *Mind in society: The development of higher psychological processes.* (M. Cole, V. John-Steiner, S. Scribner & E. Souberman, Eds. and Trans.) Cambridge, MA: Harvard University Press. (Original work published 1934)

Wade, S.E. & Moje, E.B. (2000) "The role of text in classroom learning." In M. L. Kamil, P. B. Mosenthal, P. D. Pearson, & R. Barr (eds.), *Handbook of reading research* (Vol. 3, 609–627). Mahwah, NJ: Erlbaum.

Wiggins, G. & McTighe, J. (2000) *Understanding by design.* Alexandria, VA: ASCD.

Wilhelm, J. (2002) *Action strategies for deepening comprehension.* New York, NY: Scholastic.

Wilhelm, J. (2007) *Engaging readers and writers with inquiry: Promoting deep understandings in language arts and the content areas with guiding questions.* New York, NY: Scholastic.

Wilhelm, J. (2001) *Improving comprehension with think-aloud strategies.* New York, NY: Scholastic.

Wilhelm, J. (2004) *Reading is seeing.* New York, NY: Scholastic.

Wilhelm, J., Baker, N. & Dube Hackett, J. (2001) *Strategic reading: Guiding students to lifelong literacy 6–12.* Portsmouth, NH: Boynton/Cook.

Wlodkowski, R. & Ginsberg, M. (1995) "A framework for culturally responsive teaching." *Educational Leadership, 53*(1), 17–21.

Zimmerman, B.J. & Schunk, D.H. (2001) "Reflections on theories of self-regulated learning and academic achievement." In. B. J. Zimmerman & D. H. Schunk (eds.) *Self-regulated learning and academic achievement: Theoretical perspectives* (2nd ed., 289–307). Mahwah, NJ: Erlbaum.

Index